Collages

A Jewish Girl's Search for Self

by

Sharon Levine Yedwab

ISBN: 0-7596-3195-6

This book is printed on acid free paper.

1stBooks – rev. 02/25/02

Disclaimer

This is a work of fiction. All names, places, and situations contained in this novel are either products of the author's imagination or used in a fictitious manner. Any similarity to actual persons, living or dead, places, or situations is coincidental.

Dedicated
To
My
Family and Friends

About the Author

Sharon Levine Yedwab holds a BA in Psychology from Boston University and an MAT in British and American Literature from Rutgers University. She teaches English and Reading in Passaic High School, Passaic, New Jersey, where she has directed a Summer Theater Workshop and is advisor to the Poetry/Reading Club. Mrs. Yedwab also facilitates a series of Passaic High School Multicultural Poetry Workshops, and has edited several collections of student poetry, entitled, *Walking in Someone Else's Shoes Volumes I and II* and *Multicultural Poetry for the Millennium*. She lives in West Orange, New Jersey with her husband, and has three children.

Mark Seglin, Ph.D., licensed psychologist and certified psychoanalytic psychotherapist, who served as a consultant for the therapy scenes in the novel, holds a private practice in Newark, New Jersey.

CHAPTER 1

The Jersey City gym was hot with high ceilings and aging equipment. Men, mostly over forty, wearing sweatbands around balding heads, hurtled themselves around an ancient track. Marty Zemmel, a psychiatrist in his early fifties with piercing eyes, generous lips and a quiet unassuming air that belied the size and strength of his frame, enjoyed the decrepit ambiance away from the trendy suburbs. An amateur boxer in his youth, he no longer entered the ring, but still prized a trim body and clung to the hope that fitness, or even an attempt at it, would alleviate the bouts of upper respiratory ailments he suffered lately.

The thrill of the adrenaline rush and the feeling of his heart pounding in his chest were a welcome relief from the abstractions of psychiatry. In the gym, Marty escaped from the cerebral grind where he supported patients in their painful struggles to decode seemingly incomprehensible puzzles of existence. Here, he was a man of action, not a problem solver. His stance as eternal listener was pushed aside, while he punched his own fantasies into the bag. The stoic bag was the respected standard in the gym, and Marty made love to it with his fists.

During these workouts, Marty obliterated all thought of advancing age, insurance companies, a recalcitrant son and a wife who no longer excited him. He was completely immersed in this ancient arena, amidst the acrid stench of sweaty bodies catapulted to the limit of physical endurance. His office, filled with books on the latest secrets concerning psychological labyrinths, was thrashed into oblivion while he prayed diligently for a second wind.

But today's impromptu workout was different. There were thoughts that resisted pounding, and feelings he couldn't subdue. They tugged at him as he searched for reasons to explain His presence at the gym. Why the hell aren't you at work, exploded

1

a voice he sought to deny. Yet, he couldn't suppress his arousal at the thought of her name.

Once more, Marty pictured Bliss with her shiny black hair, vulnerable dark eyes and slender figure on that fateful afternoon in Central Park. He was his wife's replacement in a bike-a-thon to support Russian Jewry and Bliss was just out for Sunday exercise. How was it, he wondered, that she lost her footing and fell from her bike at the very moment that he crossed her path? And then he recalled the look of endearing helplessness he glimpsed in her, and how she tried to hide it. She even rejected his extended hand at first.

"Thanks, I can handle it," she mumbled.

"I'm a doctor," he coaxed.

"But I don't know you," she insisted.

Why was her vulnerability so attractive to him, he wondered, and realized the answer lay in his own wounds that never healed.

When he saw her sprawled beside her bike, rubbing her elbow, with no clear idea of how to get up, Marty was transported to a time when he was seven years old. His new bike gave him a sense of pride he never knew before, and he enjoyed showing off. One day he set up a ramp that would attract all the neighborhood kids. The excitement was momentous, and Marty never saw the rock. He never saw the rock someone purposely put in his way, and was more hurt by the laughter than the physical bruises. He wanted someone to kiss him and make it better, but he was too ashamed to even tell his mom. And now this woman, whose age he guessed as thirtyish, lay before him, and in her eyes, Marty saw all the helplessness he ever experienced.

Marty extended his hand once more, "My name's Marty Zemmel."

She gave in to his persistence and took his hand. "Bliss Rothstein," she began, and half rose, but a twinge in her elbow made Bliss inhale sharply. She lost her balance and lurched against Marty. He was surprised to feel her weight on him and enjoyed her warmth. He noticed a responsiveness that invited intimacy. There was a mystery to her and he wanted to explore it. He wanted to caress her, possibly make love with her.

His encircling arm no longer steadied her, but embraced her. Smells of summer's grass and flowers blended with his strength, creating an unforgettable mosaic for Bliss, and she kissed him. "I never kissed a doctor before," she murmured. Instantaneously, a lifetime of calculation and manipulation fell apart for Marty.

Marty always fought hard for control. He grew up in an Italian section of the Bronx where he was perpetually on guard. Marty was often disliked, usually smaller, and obnoxiously smarter than his classmates, but his final affirmation of isolation was his Jewishness. Fortunately, he competed with his fists as well as his head, so he eventually earned the respect of his peers, although never their friendship. Close familiarity was very remote in his early years, which compelled the boy to embrace discipline as the next best way of life. If he couldn't fit into the environment, he would at least manipulate it. Life for Marty was a problem that always bore a solution. Sometimes it came by fist, but usually he employed his mind.

No one who knew Marty from the old neighborhood was surprised at his dual love of boxing and psychiatry. What did surprise them was his complete lack of bitterness. Rather than hating the guys, Marty never lost his wish to be one of them. He protested their bigotry and this empowered his drive to fight for the underdog. During college, and long after that, Marty steadfastly wanted to make a dent in the overwhelming unhappiness and unfairness he saw everywhere.

This was precisely why he hated himself in the gym that afternoon in late summer. He was capitulating, and the last vestiges of idealism were almost gone. Now at midlife, he contemplated an extramarital affair. Order was only a myth, dying a not so slow death. His wife's crow's feet loomed large in front of him. G-d, how she abhorred them. Creams and mud packs scattered all over her bathroom were now framed in his consciousness as a new sensation gripped him. The usual lack of interest in his wife was evolving into something ugly.

"You don't think I'm attractive," she accused him that morning, which pierced the veneer of their usually stoic relationship.   He knew she was hurt by his recent disappearances, and became unnerved.

"Aging's been rough on both of us," he finally answered. "I'm sorry I've had to spend so much time at the hospital lately," he added.   "Lombardi's been out with a gall bladder operation and I've been handling his cases for him."

She shot him a look of disbelief. His stab at an explanation sounded like an admission of guilt to her.

He punched the hurt he knew Anne felt into the bag in front of his face. Quick staccato jabs encouraged him to envision an even sadder version of his wife. Tears mingled with crow's feet, as he pictured Anne's loneliness. He was never really there for her, yet she continually accepted it. All those long nights in his career building days were the price she paid for the prestige he later enjoyed.

But she enjoyed your position, the bag punched back, and his arm paused in mid-swing. In fact, his arm formed a perfect arc as the next thought hit him. How do I really know her feelings are more genuine than mine? And, before he could recover, the bag hit him with a final death blow. Perhaps she's already cheating. Impossible, he countered with a limp punch which missed the mark. Possible, returned the bag smartly. Wasn't he about to embark on a venture never contemplated before?   Wasn't he compelled into action by his frustration? Thoughts of frustration loosened him as he lovingly battered the bag. It was actually a relief to diminish Anne and the feelings she still might harbor for him. It took the sting out of the humiliation he read in her crow's feet, her more than occasional drink and the stretch marks on her belly that bore their only son.

Marty was desperate to confide in someone, but there was no one he dared entrust with his dilemma. The intensity of his isolation was unbearable which was why he was at the gym rather than at work. He needed to resolve his issues before they destroyed him, but although the punching bag eased his anxiety, it did not diminish it. With three days worth of stubble on his face, Marty finally allowed himself to realize, that he was on a dangerous precipice with a magnificent view, that he did not want to lose. Convention was stifling him, and after an hour's worth of slugging it out with himself, Marty was forced to confront just how made up his mind actually was. Values were smashed and deception was imminent. He read his betrayal of Anne in neon signs everywhere he looked, but Marty knew his very betrayal was a passport to fulfillment of his inner life. Feeling more confident than he had in weeks, and without a backward glance at anyone, Marty left the gym without any further hesitation. He finally realized this was a journey he would have to make.

Marty hungered for the woman whose very name embodied exactly what he sought, and was consumed by a desire to be in her intensely cluttered upper West Side apartment. His car was dangerously over the speed limit in the Holland Tunnel when Marty recalled fragments of an earlier conversation.

"I'm divorced. I live with my son," she confided. "What about you?"

"I also have a son," he hedged.

"And?"

"And I'm married."

There was silence. "Thanks for telling me the truth," she said. "Maybe we won't hurt each other if we're honest."

Marty wasn't so sure, as he drove towards her apartment. He pursued her because she offered him the excitement he craved whether or not the game was fair. Perhaps some of that excitement is to hurt her, he mused.

*   *   *   *

Bliss's crowded five room rent controlled apartment, considered large by New Yorkers, was bursting with what many would call junk. Yet to Bliss, who lived like the eye of the hurricane, the apartment was not chaotic. Rather, it contained the essentials necessary to the existence of her small family. What appeared like clutter to strangers was really what it took for them to live. Everything down to the last pile of charity envelopes screaming for help from all over the world, along with bills waiting to be paid, was in its proper place.

To Marty it felt like home. Bliss's ability to cope with what appeared incoherent soothed him. He was most absorbed by the cluttered chaos, which started in the kitchen and spilled into the rest of the apartment. Marty found the overabundance of papers, books, plants, sheet music, toys, mostly unhung paintings and cheap knickknacks, collected from anywhere Bliss and her son traveled, a welcome escape from the sterility of his suburban mini-mansion.

That afternoon Marty climbed the backstairs of Bliss's apartment after she buzzed him in. He took the stairs because elevators, especially small apartment elevators, made him nervous. Her cooking wafted down to him and he was reminded of his medical school days, as he was on his first visit. Strange that we both took the day off, he thought to himself as he heard her unlocking the chains.

When Bliss answered the door, she could not forget that he was married. Be sophisticated, she admonished herself, and smiled at Marty. Neither one said anything and it was slightly awkward.

"Where's your son?" he asked.

"With his father," she answered.

Bliss purposely did not ask Marty about his son and moved to the stove, glad to check the rice. Almost burning her hand, she was acutely aware of her vulnerability.

6

"Look," she said with her back to him, "if this is going to be awful, let's cut it off right now."

Though he spied the out he possibly sought, Marty didn't take it. He was desperate to heal his own emptiness and eschewed traditional values.

"You're right," he said, meeting her at the stove and placing his hand on her neck. "Let's not talk shop."

"What then?"

"Let's talk poetry."

"You mean feelings," she trembled.

"That's it," he whispered into her breasts and noted their vibrancy in comparison to his wife's sagging flesh.

They finally kissed and experienced the intimacy they both craved. Bliss and Marty undressed each other in the shadows of the kitchen and lay down on the not-too-clean floor. The cool tiles made the experience more authentic for them as they shunned convention.

Marty moved hypnotically. Exalting in his subtlety, Bliss relaxed into a compatible rhythm. She sensed passion in him and liked the way his urgency made her own sexuality come alive. Her small, firm breasts were very beautiful to him, as he traced them with gentle fingers, and then he was happily lost in her. All else faded. Their arms and legs entwined in naked ecstasy, Bliss swallowed his spice. Lovemaking brought them closer. No longer lonely, they slept.

Bliss was the first to hear the sound of Marty's beeper coming from the clothes heaped beside them. She immediately panicked, sure it was a fire.

"No, no, it's my beeper," he mumbled, groping for it in a semi-fog. "Where's the phone?"

"On the wall near the door," she casually pointed to the other end of the room.

When Marty picked up the receiver, he heard nothing.

"There's no dial tone here," he called over his shoulder. "This thing's dead as a door knob. The line must be down. My cell phone's in the car. I'll be back in a few."

Reality crashed on Bliss. "Can't all this wait?" she questioned without much hope.

"I'm afraid not," answered Marty, already reaching for his shirt; not perceiving her mood. "It's the hospital."

Romance diminished quickly and Bliss noticed the cold harshness of the floor. Her back ached and nakedness turned into embarrassment. She pulled on a sweater and boiled some water for coffee, the uneaten meal no longer appealing. She sat down by the table and cradled her head in her arms, unable to fend off feelings of disappointment.

Marty lightly kissed her on the shoulder. "Keep the food warm."

Bliss never heard the door shut. She absentmindedly doodled at the kitchen table, pulling her knees up to her chest. A short time ago it was so warmly intimate and now, as usual, she was left alone. Even though Marty seemed different, she detected the same old pattern of abandonment. Only the excuses varied.

Now on the street, Marty headed for his car and shoved aside feelings that told him to run. He dialed several times before he was able to reach the hospital. Inevitably, it was the saddest emergency—a teenage suicide attempt.

"We can handle it 'til morning," said the seasoned nurse on the phone. "However, her parents want you to call them after 10:00."

"Thanks, I'll take the information now," said Marty, who glanced at his watch and noticed it was only 9:30.

Marty stared at the phone number. What can I tell this man, Ed Levy, he wondered. What can I ever tell parents? And then his professionalism took over. He reminded himself that it was never what he could tell anyone. Rather, it was what they told *him* that mattered. But how to find the right words to get them to talk, he asked himself, as he unconsciously headed towards Bliss.

Zemmel contemplated the array of events as he once again trudged up the stairs to the apartment. First there was the interruption with Bliss, then the dead phone, and now a suicide attempt. A dabbler in Jewish mysticism, Zemmel often wondered about how things worked beneath the surface. He meditated as he climbed the final stairs and thought about the dead phone, noting that it matched the deadness he struggled with lately.

When Marty attempted to enter the apartment and reestablish his earlier intimacy with Bliss, she was resistant. Her earlier warmth gone, she assaulted him with a barrage of questions in relation to his phone call. He explained that his work at the hospital was confidential, and expected her to react similarly to his wife, who respected his privacy. But Bliss refused to retreat. Her insecurity wouldn't allow secrets.

"I never want to hear that damned beeper again."

"I'm a doctor," he offered, without much conviction.

"Fuck being a doctor," she fumed and slammed the door in his face.

. . . .

"Mr. Levy....hello, this is Dr. Zemmel. I was referred to treat your daughter by your family physician."

"Oh, Dr. Zemmel, hello," stalled Levy, desperately sorting through fragmentation. "I think my wife and I overreacted. We just put our daughter into the hospital. She's our only daughter, you know. How can we be home while she's in the hospital?"

"Hmmm," responded Zemmel, immediately recognizing the challenge of Levy's denial.

"It was the blood that scared us. It was pouring like a water faucet. I guess you know she slit her wrists."

"So why do you think you overreacted?"

"Hospitals are for the mentally ill, severely disturbed, nonfunctional individuals. My daughter is a beautiful young woman. She's not sick."

"It sounds as though you love your daughter a great deal," soothed Zemmel in gentle tones.

"I do love her, Doctor. We both do, and that's what's tearing us apart," sobbed Levy. "My daughter was dripping with blood. I let it happen. She needed me and I wasn't there."

Silently, Zemmel caught his breath. This was more than a parent venting guilty frustration. Levy was ready to share.

"Andi was too involved with a boy from school. I knew she was floundering, but I turned away and made believe she was still my baby."

"Can you tell me something about this involvement?"

"The boy wasn't Jewish. I didn't really mind, but for my wife it became a battle of nerves, a cold war."

"It sounds like we're dealing with some very strong personalities," said Zemmel, trying to engage Ed into further introspection. But even Marty's most professional tones were not enough to make Ed delve any deeper into his wound. For a moment both men were silent, and then the line clicked off in Marty's ear.

CHAPTER 2

The room was a dingy green and white. Discolored shades covered the windows, allowing the faintest ray of sunlight to fall on the gray linoleum. There was a blood stain on the ceiling directly above a single chest of drawers and diagonally across from a narrow cot. A straight cane-backed chair completed Andi Levy's view.

Actually, this room afforded no privacy, as it was merely partitioned off from a larger area, an observation center where Andi was placed during the night. She slept an exhausted sleep, relatively unaware of her new environment.

The quiet of the hospital was soon broken by early morning activity, and Andi was jolted to consciousness.

"Wake up! We don't sleep late here."

Her eyes opened and then automatically shut against unhappy memories. But the hand on her shoulder was insistent and she finally opened her eyes against her will. She examined her fuzzy surroundings and managed to focus on the attendant.

"I need a hug," she blurted.

"We don't do that here. Come on, it's time to wash up."

Weakly, Andi tried to prop herself up on the cot, but immediately fell backward. "I'm tired, I can't," she groaned.

"Well, we'll see about that," said the attendant, who slowly moved away. "Your doctor will be in to examine you soon."

"Wait," called Andi, in growing desperation, "I need to go to the bathroom."

Andi stared at the walls and ceiling, waiting for the attendant to return. Her eyes finally riveted on the blood stain and she froze.

"Where'd that come from?" she inquired through her fear.

"Look, I'll help you get to the lav," said the attendant, pointedly ignoring her question.

She recalled little from the night before as she slowly clutched the white-clothed arm. Anxious to replace inner horror with the details of reality, she pressed further.

"Please, I'm just trying to remember..."

As he steered her to the bathrooms, the attendant was professionally firm.

"That's for you to discuss with your doctor."

Andi stood before a rather large lavatory without fully realizing how she got there. Even from the outside, she saw that none of the stalls had doors.

"Go on in. I'll wait for you," urged the attendant.

Andi found it impossible to urinate, even though her bladder was full. She grew cold watching patients walk back and forth. Never exposed like this before, she told herself to breathe deeply and to gain control.

Eventually she relaxed and imagined herself with Joe. But her reverie ended quickly with thoughts of his betrayal. She desperately reached for anything familiar and remembered their favorite song. But her anxiety worsened with the lyrics, and her breathing became irregular. She saw her life as a cruel joke and then everything went blank.

Moments later she found herself on the floor. Her forehead was pressed into bathroom tile and there was an awful scent in her nose. Andi heard words in the distance.

"Fainted, she fainted..."

"I...I'm all right. What happened? Did I...?"

She touched urine on the bathroom tiles beneath her and all dignity was lost. At that moment it felt like a losing battle. Her head dropped to the floor once more.

"Come on, I'll wash you off," said the attendant. "That's right. That's the girl."

Andi let him handle her, while she remained uncharacteristically docile and cooperated only in response to the fear that gripped her heart.

Breakfast carts clanged in the morning meal as Andi returned to her cot. Noise of tin ware against plastic plates began, while coffee sloshed from huge urns. Rather than food, someone handed her a metal container to place under her chin. Almost gratefully, she retched.

The nightmarish muddle of the previous night began to unravel when she banged her head, so Andi tried hard to avoid deeper thought. She forced herself to think only of the dreadful bitter taste in her mouth, carefully averting her eyes from the blood on the ceiling. Hunched over, she drifted into sleep without enough strength to demand water.

Once more there was a hand on her shoulder. But this time the shake seemed gentler, even friendly. Instead of a white-coated arm, it was someone in a business suit. Andi let her eyes explore the walls, rather than look at him. Finally she focused on the chair and remembered her thirst.

"I need water," croaked Andi through parched lips.

"O.K., I'll have the nurse get you some."

Andi took a drink and finally looked at him.

"Hi, do you know who I am?" he asked cheerfully.

How should I know, I never saw you before, she thought to herself. "Are you the doctor...the psychiatrist?" she finally guessed. "What's your name?"

"Well, the plaque in my office says I'm Dr. Zemmel," he chuckled.

She didn't like the joke and turned to the wall.

"Thanks for the drink," she mumbled.

"Mind if I sit down?" he asked, and pulled the chair over to her cot.

She didn't answer him.

"I heard you had a nasty spill this morning. Does your head hurt?" he continued after a pause.

Her tongue felt thick in her mouth and she struggled fiercely for lucidity.

"What do you think?" she spoke into the wall.

"Would you like me to look at it? I am a doctor."

She turned onto her back.

"Good...I'll take that as a yes," he said, feeling the bump on her forehead. "So what do you think of the accommodations?"

"I don't like the toilets."

"Yeah, it's hard getting used to no doors."

She said nothing. Sensitive to her acute vulnerability, he decided to stop probing. His voice softened as he picked up his note pad.

"Take care of yourself. I'll be back tomorrow. It's lunch time. Try the food."

Andi ignored his departure and turned back to the wall as she attempted to shut out the clang of the lunch carts along with the smell of lunch itself.

CHAPTER 3

"I'm sorry, but you can't go in there. You're under observation," said someone in white.

"What do you mean?" asked Andi in amazement.

"Those are the doctor's orders."

"What doctor? I've barely seen anyone."

"He was just here this morning. Don't you remember?"

"Look, I just want to make a phone call."

"I understand. But the phone's in an area that's off limits for you right now. Doctor's orders."

"Please, give me a break. I really need to use the..."

"Look Hon, just settle down. I think your doctor will be here very soon."

"Screw the doctor! I just want..."

"I'm very sorry dear, but until you get permission you'll just have to stay near your cot."

"What about the bathroom?"

"Someone will take you."

Andi's throat and chest constricted in a suffocating choke. Further realization of her confinement brought tears of anger and frustration to her eyes. She was penned in like an animal and hated it. Alone and trapped, she attempted to prevail against fear. If only she could talk to Joe, she was sure he would help. She told herself to breathe in and out.

'Come on, get a grip. Breathe. I know I can do this!'

All too well, she recognized there were no second chances for her here. There were only secret unbearable rooms, all green and gray and white. Everything frightened her and hysteria mounted. She forgot to concentrate on breathing. Fixated on making the phone call, Andi inched closer to forbidden territory, and managed to slip away from the nurses station. But the nurse, quite skilled at handling situations like these, quickly steered Andi back to her cot.

15

Andi turned to the wall, defeated. Her arms hugged her legs in a knot, as her fingernails drew blood from her flesh. She knew her head was banging against the wall, but didn't care. Control all but forgotten, she pushed any possible existing remnant away. In fact, she liked the banging. It filled her up deep inside, where she could feel it and hear it and scream it all at once. She was banging and she was the bang, finally in harmony. Hands and feet and face and head, all in concert, banged against the wall; while plaster, paint, hair, blood and flesh merged into oblivion. As she pounded the wall with every inch of her strength, she issued a blood-curdling animal sound that filled her space. It was the only sound she wanted to hear, and gradually the bang inside fulfilled itself.

Hands were upon her, cruelly pulling and pushing, but she wouldn't let go. Rather, she clawed and hugged the wall, inhaling green plaster as if it was her only food; her final support. And then she was on her back, completely still.

Her face was a map of rage and despair and she never wanted to look at anyone again. She was unbearably aware of her exposure, her loss of humanity, her utter humiliation and hoped that no one would ever look at her. But awareness was distanced. Rational thoughts were pushed far away by other much more powerful forces. Andi made no attempt to discipline the anger and despair ravaging her psyche. She gave up responsibility for herself because she believed she was powerless in the wake of unbridled emotion.

Andi's confidence and self-esteem eroded, she allowed others to put their judgment above her own. From across the murky abyss, the strait jacket that now imprisoned her upper body was hurtful and humiliating, but she accepted it as necessary attire to her devastated body. She considered it a reply to her scream; a direct answer to her cry. In no uncertain terms, she knew that no one listened to her from the inside, and so she went limp.

Andi lay on her back with her arms pulled round her upper body and was desperate for water. She breathed with difficulty and raised her head a fraction to call for help. But when she saw people who didn't see her, her entreaties appeared useless, so she gave up and let her head fall back on the pillow. Sure she was forgotten in the hubbub of activity centered around the clanging meal carts bringing supper, she was startled by a voice...

"I'll send someone over to help you eat."

"I'm not hungry."

"Come on now. It'll be easier to eat than you think. Anyway, tonight's one of our better meals."

"How long will I..."

"Have to wear that?"

"Yeah."

"Well, that really depends on you."

"It's cutting into my shoulder."

"Hmmm, that's pretty common. Later on you'll get some salve."

"I really need to see the doctor."

"I know, Hon. He should be by to see you tomorrow. Just try to relax."

"Can I have some water? My throat's really dry."

"In a minute. You'll get it with supper."

"But I'm..."

"You'll just have to wait. I'm very busy right now."

Andi reclined on the cot, despondently sliding her toe against the wall. She was forced to tap resources never used before, as she envisioned herself an abandoned sack of potatoes. At first, breathing appeared impossible.

"I can't breathe. I'm choking to death," she cried softly to herself.

But gradually strength took hold and she began coping with an exercise she remembered from a yoga class. Breathe deeply. Breathe in, breathe out. Take the air in. Let it out...she almost could hear the instructor's words.

17

Slowly, inch by inch, she brought thought and feeling under restraint, but control was fleeting. In her fantasy, she pictured herself tied up in a claustrophobic knot with no arms. She was managed by others, while fear subdued strength. As she pursued her thoughts, she discovered a gentle softness, very fragile; very vulnerable.

Andi delved further and further into feeling, losing all interest in space and time, and embraced new-found softness. Wrapped arms hugged body heat in a fight against loneliness, as her head rhythmically pounded the pillow. Her head moved violently; head up, head down, head up, head down, pound, pound, pound. From inside, the sound of the pound, the feel of the pound, the cry of the pound was perfect. The screams from twisted body, heart, and mouth expressed her utter agony. "I can't get out. Let me out. Out! Out! Let me out...out of here now!"

Words from the angry struggle within and without reverberated against pillow, wall and ceiling as her body arched in seizure.

Hands again! Hands, hands, hands were all over, pulling her, pushing her, shoving her. Controlling hands, saving hands, impersonal hands subdued her, all pummeling at the intimacy of her heart.

"There now, that's better. That's the girl. Just rest. That's right. Breathe in. Breathe out. That's the girl. Your shoulder looks a little red. We'll get some salve in a minute. Meantime, you just relax."

She smoldered in a puddle of sweat and urine, her tortured body ravaged by the tantrum, and concentrated on the designs of the peeling plaster next to her bed. They looked like monsters ready to attack her while she was all alone. She felt so small struggling on a cot with tied arms, where there was nothing but hospital wall and pillow and jacket and people drawing lines she dared not overstep. Keep away, she wanted to shout, but no words came. Soon she tired of the cracks in the wall and her eyes turned completely inward. Body spent, heart finally silent, breathing slowed, her eyelids closed in sleep.

CHAPTER 4

The fury of Andi's chaos mildly jarred the staff from their usual callousness. When Mary came in for evening duty, Madi called her aside.

"Listen," she said, pointing to the cot on the left wall of the observation area, "that one's had a rough day. She wasn't able to take food. I put some supper aside for her in case she wakes up hungry during the night."

"What about her meds?"

"Thorazine. She's barely seen her doctor."

"Who is he?"

"Zemmel. He's pretty good, but it's always the same. We end up doing everything. She got so bad we put her in a jacket and gave her a shot of Prolixin. By the way, she may need some salve for her left shoulder. It's pretty raw."

Together they walked over to the girl lying in crumpled exhaustion. Mary was immediately drawn to her.

"G-d, she looks small. How old is she?"

"Sixteen."

"What's her name?"

"Andrea Levy."

"Why did she flip out?"

"I'm really not sure. Something about wanting to use the phone."

Laughing in a friendly way, Mary conjectured, "It's always like that. It's never anything but little pieces of nonsense."

"Maybe that's why they call it a nut house."

"Could be any house, I guess."

Mary enjoyed the night shift. The place was huge and quiet, and in the stark barn-like atmosphere, she experienced total control. Everything was in complete order. Except for the restless shadows of the sleepers projecting their macabre dance on the walls, nothing moved. Mary felt a sacred oneness with

20

the patients as she moved from room to room, bed to bed on her hourly rounds and practiced a mantra she learned at a continuing education class. She meditated on the health of the inmates, hoping that sleep would provide a cure beyond medication.

Mary was outgoing and concerned with her patients and she sometimes wondered what they were like before their illnesses. Some of them were quite rich and others were famous in various ways. What brought them all together, she often speculated. Was the only focal point mental illness, or was there a deeper nexus, a more significant meaning to the lives of the spiritually tortured? As a recovered alcoholic, Mary was able to push aside the hospital cynicism and nurture a belief that there was a hidden meaning to human tragedy. She gravitated to Andi's cot to investigate the girl defined only as the new patient, the one in the jacket.

Mary stared down at Andi whose arms were caught like the wings of a trapped bird and was struck by her physical slightness once again. Silently, she watched Andi tossing back and forth in sleep, as a low moan issued through the girl's body. Experience told Mary the patient might soon awaken, so she hurriedly read her chart.

Mary looked for clues to a patient's humanity, when she read charts. She sought to heal rather than label, and usually noted what was omitted. As she read the description of Andi's telephone episode, Mary realized it wasn't as trivial as it first sounded. Oddly, there was no mention of who the girl wanted to call. Why was this call so important to her, wondered Mary. Maybe there were powerful reasons behind Andi's rage. There were too many unanswered questions to determine whether the behavior was actually psychotic, yet the patient was on a heavy regime of antipsychotic medication, observed Mary with disgust.

Andi awakened ravenously thirsty and reflexively yanked her jacket. She raised her hand and almost tipped the cot while she croaked for attention. Mary reached for a carafe and poured her young patient some water.

"The medication's probably making you thirsty," she said gently.

Andi remembered her shoulder only after a long gulp of water.

"My shoulder's burning me."

"O.K....lean back and I'll get some salve."

Andi hated being left alone by the nurse. Every muscle in her body ached. Her mind was numb and her head throbbed like a blister. The fire in her shoulder made it hard to lie still and she longed for escape. But with barely enough energy to wiggle her toes, she knew it was impossible. Fighting the fear that choked her, Andi imagined she was on the ceiling looking down at her own shadow. Who is this girl? How did she get here? Why does she exist at all? Using all her willpower, Andi brought herself down from the ceiling without really knowing why.

Mary returned to find Andi huddled in a ball, with knees up against pretzel arms. The sight of such frailty motivated Mary to reach out and hug the girl. But almost immediately she remembered never to touch patients and stopped herself. Instead, she used her most comforting voice.

"Lean over, Andrea, and I'll put on some salve."

Surprised at her patient's lack of response, Mary tried again.

"Turn to the side, Andrea, so I can make your shoulder feel better."

Andi still refused to budge. Mary opened her mouth to coax once more, but closed it sharply. After all, as Madi said earlier, this was a nut house. Mary was all too used to the irrational, and simply turned to leave. However, the ear-splitting scream that came from the cot froze her instantly.

"Don't call me by that name."

Half turning to gain control, Mary wondered what the problem was. The chart said her name was Andrea and that's what Madi called her.

"What would you like me to call you?" she asked quietly.

Andi didn't answer, so Mary attempted to respond to the girl's needs without further provocation.

"Would you like some salve?" she asked tonelessly.

Andi's sobs prompted Mary to turn around completely, but still wary of the girl's reaction, she waited for a signal before moving forward. Tears streamed down Andi's face. She desperately wanted the nurse's attention and was afraid she might leave again. So the girl searched for words.

"Please help me," she whispered. "I'm sorry I yelled at you, but I hate my name."

CHAPTER 5

"Good morning."

The sun was shining brightly when Andi opened her eyes. The sight of the doctor in front of her made her forget the terrible ache in her arms for just a moment. In the same instant, she noticed something was missing. Where were the breakfast carts, she wondered.

Aloud, she asked, "What time is it?"

"Ten o'clock."

"What happened? No one sleeps late here. Did they forget to wake me up?

Smiling at her, Zemmel pulled up a chair and seemed proud to take credit.

"Doctor's orders."

Andi allowed herself to share his good humor, but panicked almost immediately, sensing trap doors she didn't want to open. In an effort to coax back the half-formed smile, Zemmel continued his cheerfulness.

"I've ordered you a late breakfast."

When the girl failed to respond, he tentatively used her name, "Andrea."

Her answer was to hunch over; knees up, shoulders down, arms twisted behind her back.

He regarded her silently, sure more was coming.

"Don't call me Andrea. I hate her. I hate me."

"Say more about hate."

"Hate, hate," she screamed, "I hate everyone. They hate me. Leave me alone."

Itchy and sweaty, she awkwardly swung herself to the wall. She didn't want him to go, but she couldn't face him. She wanted to talk, but words were distant. Andi dreaded the passing time and feared he would go before she said anything. Applying no pressure, Zemmel waited. Andi finally broke her silence in reaction to his.

"Get me out of this," she yelled, shaking her upper body at the wall.

While he continued staring at her, she struggled for fragments of control and found a softer voice.

"Please, I'm ready to come out."

Zemmel choked back a cough and reached inside his pocket for a cough drop.

"You mean you're ready to come out of restraint?"

Calmer, she nodded and Zemmel summoned an attendant.

The attendant undid the restraints. Andi's numb arms unfolded inch by inch; it felt good to be free. She cradled her punished arms with tingling fingers, while she gratefully looked at the doctor and shyly waited for him to speak. When he didn't, she felt surprisingly cheated.

"You don't care about me," she complained, but he still said nothing.

Dismayed by his stare, Andi sought his sympathy.

"Well, say something," she pleaded.

His continued lack of response maddened her.

"Why don't you talk? What do you want me to say?" Andi exploded.

"Anything that comes to mind," Zemmel finally answered.

"I told you before, you don't care about me."

"Say more about caring."

"What's there to say? Nobody cares."

Again, he said nothing. His silence, aggravating at first, systematically loosened her words.

"Who says anyone has to care? I don't care, so why should they?" exclaimed Andi.

"Tell me more about who *they* are."

"Why, what do you want to know?"

"Who are they? What are they like?"

"They're my parents."

"Mm."

"'Specially my mother; I hate her. She hates me!"

"And?"

"And nothing; zip, zero, finished."

"Say more."

"More, why should I? I'm sure you've spoken with them. What more do you want?"

"I'm here to speak with you. Everything we say is confidential. I'm going to be your doctor for a while. What you think and feel is important."

"Oh, so you can figure out the right pills to give me?"

"Not necessarily. Actually, I prefer giving therapy."

In school, Andi occasionally heard of someone, never anyone popular, who was in therapy. It never sounded very attractive. In fact, it was something she really didn't want to consider. But now with Dr. Zemmel, it didn't sound so alarming. Truthfully, she was very curious.

"I wonder if people care for each other in therapy," she looked at him closely. This time, his silence didn't hurt so much and, after a brief pause, she continued.

"Is it O.K. for me to care for you?"

"Yes, it's O.K.," he said gently, "but I'm afraid our time is up for today. We'll talk again tomorrow. By the way, your late breakfast is coming."

He rose to leave and panic erupted inside her. It was impossible. He couldn't go yet.

"Stay," she screeched. Her echo reverberated against walls and ceiling. Desperately, her hands clutched the sides of the cot and the backs of her heels dug into the mattress, but she didn't lose further control. Rather, she held on to new, half-formed thoughts about therapy. She sniffed the pancakes from the breakfast tray, and for the first time in a while eating seemed like a good idea.

CHAPTER 6

As she lay on her cot after breakfast, Andi gradually relaxed, and indulged in a daydream. The shrink was kind of cute for an older guy. He reminded her of her 10th grade English teacher, the one who directed the school play. But reminiscing about the play was leading into dangerous territory, and unsure of where to go with it, she distracted herself by peeling the green plaster on the wall. Chips began falling on her jeans as she loosened plaster with her fingers. This time, the chips didn't look like monsters, but she thought she saw red in them. Red, she panicked, that could be blood—my blood. And it's getting all over my pants. I've got to get out of them, she thought, starting to freeze inside. But where are my clothes?

Andi had no idea where her suitcase was and started gagging. Just then she heard a tap on her dresser.

"Hello, my name is Rose. How are you?" asked a thin, intense woman.

Andi was sure the woman was there because of the blood and didn't know how to respond.

"I need to talk to you," continued the woman in an accent that sounded vaguely familiar to Andi.

"Why? Because I'm bloody? It's not my fault," Andi protested. "I can't remember where my clothes are and this paint looks like blood. Does the blood smell? Who are you anyway?"

"I'm sorry," said Rose, aware of a communication gap. "I guess I didn't properly introduce myself. My name is Rose Schneider and I'm a social worker here at the hospital. More importantly, I'm here to talk to you about our educational program for anyone under the age of 18."

"Do you mean school?" asked Andi, completely astounded.

"Of course! Just because you're here doesn't mean you get out of going to school," Rose smiled.

"Where is it?" asked Andi, and promised herself she wouldn't go.

"Right down that hall," responded Rose, pointing to the other end of the floor.

Sitting on the edge of her cot, head hanging and a sinking feeling in her stomach, Andi protested, "I can't go, I can't be with other..."

"Kids?" filled in the social worker. The girl nodded forlornly.

"I know that it's hard at first," said Rose more gently, "but we don't have many students, and remember, you're not alone. They're here working out problems just like you are."

"But I'm a wreck," Andi blurted. "I'm full of blood." For the first time, Rose took a really long look at the young girl in front of her.

"I don't see any blood," she said gently, "but if you're uncomfortable, why don't you change?"

"I just told you I don't know where my clothes are. Also, I need a shower. I..." Trembling, Andi gave up. Let them cart me to school like everywhere else, she thought. Andi stopped concentrating on the conversation and simply closed her eyes.

Rose discerned she was losing her client and switched gears. "Andrea," she said authoritatively, "open your eyes and get up." Rose was not cowed by Andi's silence. "Get up Andrea. I know you hear me. And don't give me any of your name business. We don't give in to that here. Why don't you look under your cot and you'll find your suitcase."

Andi slowly acknowledged Rose and reached for the suitcase.

"Now you can change your clothes," smiled Rose. "And don't forget to shower. You need it."

Andi laughed weakly from within her fog. "Can I go alone or will they beat me?"

"No one beats anyone here. Restraint is not beating. You know that. Besides which, according to your chart you have full floor privileges."

"Does that mean I can go anywhere?" asked Andi, excited for the first time.

"Anywhere on the floor."

"No one told me anything. Can I use the phone?"

"Of course. Fix yourself up and I'll see you again at lunch."

As she watched the social worker walk away, Andi's sixteen year old heart lifted and she wondered if Joe knew where she was. But in her next thought, the elevator sank, as she wondered if he cared.

CHAPTER 7

While she lugged her suitcase over to the dresser, Andi decided not to unpack because she didn't intend to be there long. She rummaged through her belongings and was disgusted with her mother. That figures, she almost said aloud, Mom would pack the things she likes and I hate. She knows I can't live without my cutoffs.

But when Andi spotted loose change, her horizons broadened. Great, now I won't have to call Joe collect, she told herself and wanted to call him immediately. However, hard won control asserted itself and she decided to take a shower first.

As Andi trudged to the bathroom armed with towel, soap, shampoo and change of clothes, she heard a skinny gray haired woman with bright eyes singing, "I did it my way." Andi vowed that would never happen to her. I'll never become like that woman, she shuddered to herself. Her pace to the bathrooms measurably quickened and Andi pledged she would not be in the hospital very long.

But once actually inside the bathrooms, Andi panicked. How should she go about taking her shower? She hated stepping on the filthy cement without thongs. The stalls were so cold and public. What if the water was freezing? Hopeless of ever getting clean, Andi helplessly watched any tiny nuances of hope disintegrate. Lost in this maze of despair, she was startled by a tap on her arm. Andi turned around to see a thin, rather tall girl with reddish long straight hair and deep set brown eyes whom she identified as an inmate. The girl looked lonely, but was nowhere as forlorn as Andi. Without a trace of shyness, she introduced herself.

"You must be the new girl. My name's Tina. I know this place is hard getting used to," she said, turning her eyes up at the bathroom, "'specially when you're not even feeling used to yourself."

"Yeah", laughed Andi weakly, grateful to speak with someone who seemed human.

"Look, they're pretty empty right now," advised Tina, hurriedly pointing to the showers. "Get in quick and I'll stand guard."

Hope leaped through Andi like an electric current, as she hastily adjusted the water, stepped into the shower and forgot about her bare feet.

"Wow, it feels great," she laughed, growing stronger with the force of the water. Just like anywhere."

"You know, it's really not as bad as you think," called Tina over the noise of the shower. "In a way, we're like family; just the inpatients, I mean."

"Family is usually something I try to get away from," replied Andi dryly.

"By the way, what's your name?" asked Tina, intuitively looking for something safe to discuss.

Andi stepped from the shower and toweled off quickly. She didn't want to lose a potential friend, but she was reticent to answer.

"My name's been a problem for me here," she finally answered.

Tina was curious rather than offended. She was lonely for friendship and tended to act motherly. Particularly drawn to someone her own age, Tina pressed for more information.

"What do you mean?" she asked curiously.

Feeling more congenial in clean jeans and tee shirt, Andi felt comfortable with this new girl who didn't seem to belong there, and told her the truth.

"I don't like my name much and at home nobody uses it. But in this place, people keep calling me Andrea and it makes me lonelier than ever. It makes me want to cry.

"Well, what do your friends call you?"

"They call me Andi," whispered Andi hesitantly.

"Why don't you just tell people in here about your nickname?" asked Tina, more baffled than ever.

"Because I really don't want anyone to get near me here. If they do, I know they'll start messing with my head and then I'll never get out.

Now Tina understood. A patient for 3 months, she recalled the fear of her adjustment period. She knew you had to stretch a lot to come to terms with yourself in the hospital. Tina was reminded of her own rawness during her initial confinement. She didn't want to frighten Andi with too many questions, so she simply said, "Well, I'll call you Andi then. Wanna go to lunch?"

Spirits up, Andi gathered her things, sensing many questions she wanted to ask bubbling inside her. When was the curfew? What was that school like? Were there boys in the class? What's therapy like? Tina must have therapy, she speculated, and decided to ask her about it. Did it really make you feel better, she mused, or did it just make you cry? Afraid of becoming too personal, she settled on the mundane.

"How long are you here?"

"About three months."

"Three months, that's a long time," gulped Andi.

"Not really," countered Tina. "Time goes by kind of fast here."

"Are you better?" asked Andi awkwardly, hearing the stupidity of her question even as the words left her mouth.

But Tina was glad to have a friend, and answered tolerantly.

"I don't know really. I never think of it as better or worse. I feel stronger than when I came, but I still don't feel strong enough to leave."

Andi was truly shocked. She couldn't imagine anyone not wanting to leave. The girls were so engrossed in their conversation they were surprised to see the lunch carts.

Andi viewed the roast beef sandwiches with mixed emotions, which was the way she looked at everything lately. She was fairly hungry, but the meat wasn't kosher. Andi immediately sensed her mother's disapproval. They only ate kosher food at home. Outside, she was forbidden to eat meat that wasn't kosher.

Andi wasn't really sure why they were kosher. Many of her other Jewish friends weren't. Her father even grumbled about it. Was there any point to it other than her mother's insistence?

Andi was particularly angry with her mother's attitude about unkosher cheese pizza. Why were they allowed to eat it in the pizzeria, but never at home? Whenever the subject came up, Andi believed her mother's ideas were hypocritical. Solutions were never reached and, when their voices became too high, Ed Levy, who didn't particularly share his wife's zeal, still told Andi to respect her mother and end things, or else. He privately agreed with his daughter, but didn't think it was worth a war with his wife. Andi sensed acquiescence rather than religious commitment in her father, and it only added to her exasperation. She was sure that her parents didn't really care what she thought. So why should I care what they think, she often asked herself while she munched on a hamburger at McDonald's with friends.

Ironically, hospital life added more pressure to Andi's existing anxiety about food. Eating unkosher meat on a daily basis was certainly worse then an occasional trip to Burger King. Worse still, her mother would surely find out.

Andi was torn. She was afraid of her mother's hurt and anger, but she was also sick of meaningless values being jammed down her throat.

She wasn't surprised that she couldn't make a decision, and didn't feel so hungry after all. Her hand reached into her pocket and felt loose change. Her stomach knotted immediately. She hated the cloud of apprehension that followed her everywhere and was almost relieved to see her social worker.

Rose was unaware that Andi was beginning to panic and was mistakenly pleased with her change of appearance.

"Well, you look much better," Rose commented brightly. "How are you feeling?"

33

"O.K. I guess."

Not picking up danger signals, Rose turned to Tina, while Andi quietly backed away.

"Where were you this morning? We missed you."

"I'm sorry," Tina said blushing, "but I was working on my journal and got lost in it. And then I found the new girl in the shower and we forgot the time talking."

Satisfied, Rose turned to go. "Well, make sure you're in class after lunch and bring Andrea with you."

"Uh, Rose..." Tina appealed to the social worker, thinking her new friend was getting lunch.

"Yes, what is it?" Rose asked, pausing.

"Andrea has a problem with her name. She doesn't like it very much."

"I know about that," said Rose wearily, "but what can we do? We have to call her something."

"She has a nickname," confided Tina.

"Well, what is it?" asked Rose, growing impatient.

"I can't say. She's shy about it. I just thought you should know. Things are kind of tough for her."

Rose nodded gratefully for the information. "Thanks, Tina; you just made my job a little easier. By the way, where is Andrea? It's almost time for class."

They scanned the dining area in earnest, but saw no sign of Andi anywhere. Unbelievably, she was missing.

CHAPTER 8

Clutching four quarters, Andi approached the pay phone. When she dialed Joe's number by heart, she got the operator.

"Eighty cents for the first three minutes, please."

"Damn it, I don't even have the right change," Andi muttered in disgust, and threw in all her money. She listened to the coins dropping in the box, while her heart pounded. Andi was so sure no one would respond, that the voice on the other end startled her.

"Hello, is Joe there?" she asked "It's Andi."

"Hold on, I'll check."

After a very long moment, the same voice was back on the phone. "I'm sorry, Joe's busy right now."

"Busy? Did you tell him who it was?"

"Yes, I did."

"But how..."

"Look, I'm sorry Andi, but that's what he said."

Andi fought hard to get the words out—her voice was a tearful whisper. "Does he know where I am?"

"Yes, Andi, he knows." Still firm, but gentler, the voice continued, "He says he'll call you sometime soon. Goodbye now."

Andi hung up without bothering to say goodbye. She was livid. How could he cut her off like this? She loved him so much, yet she meant so little to him. Despite their differences, she was sure her hospitalization would soften him. After all, he had a lot to do with it, she thought heatedly. But even now, he obviously didn't care, while she still did. The unfairness alone was a knife in her gut.

Her emotional temperature skyrocketed and her adrenaline raced. She felt an explosion of volcanic lava in her head that sent tremors through her arms and chest. She couldn't breathe. She couldn't even remember who she was, as her body succumbed to a panic attack. Her eyes locked in terror and could not focus, till in her frenzy she spotted the pies on the lunch carts. They were orderly. They were perfect. And she instantly realized that the pies were something she could utterly destroy.

Andi lunged for the first pie and threw it without thinking. As if from a distance, she saw pies flying from the lunch carts, splaying red and blue mixtures all over the walls, ceiling and floor. Her hands, face, shirt and jeans were covered with pie filling. Miraculously, she avoided leaping hands and arms from all over the ward, as her obscenities bounced back at her from everywhere. "Fuck you, shithead! Fuck you! Fuck! Fuck! Fuck!"

Andi unwittingly collided with an unseen stretcher and straddled it. Powered by sheer madness, she zoomed head first into the nurse's station, and in her wildly manic state, Andi never even felt the waiting hypodermic needle unceremoniously slammed into her butt before the world went dark.

* * * *

"Yes, this is Ed Levy. What's going on? First you tell me I can't even talk to my daughter because she's under observation, and now you tell me she's endured three violent episodes in two days. Where's her doctor? What does he say about all of this? O.K., we'll be there. I'll call my wife right now."

Ed hung up the phone with a gesture of futility and cursed his decision to put Andi in the hospital. Unable to control his fear, he pictured his daughter in a strait jacket.

I wanted to protect her from all danger. A father should protect. But how? Ed struggled with that question as he dialed his wife. Andi was his only child, his life. But since her Bat Mitzvah, he could not fathom her behavior. Suddenly, or so it seemed, his baby was mad about everything. She even hated her name and insisted on her nickname, Andi, everywhere. Ed remembered his own teen rebellion and told himself hers would pass. But he inevitably became irritated by the continual hassles between Andi and his wife, and usually found fault with Andi. When Andi tried to defend her point of view, he criticized her for raising her voice and told her to respect her mother. Now waiting for his wife to answer the phone, Ed guiltily wished he had paid more attention to what everyone was talking about instead of playing his role by rote.

"Sarah, hi, it's me. We have to be at the hospital in an hour."

"What's happened?' The choking feeling that plagued Sarah ever since her daughter was taken to the hospital worsened with her husband's words.

"I'm not exactly sure." For the sake of his wife's sensibility, Ed tried to be casual, but knew it was a hopeless task. "She's had an episode of some sort," he finally admitted.

"Episode? What kind of episode?" Sarah desperately gasped for air. "What exactly do you mean by episode?"

This time Ed was blunt, "I mean she lost control. I mean they sedated her."

His honesty opened the door to hers and Sarah voiced her greatest fear, "She didn't try another..." Her voice cracked and words wouldn't follow.

"No Sarah," said Ed more gently. "No one said anything about that. Now pull yourself together. We have to meet in room 410, Dr. Zemmel's office."

Sarah was terrified of hospitals—their floors, rooms, and the people in them. How was she supposed to dress to go to the hospital? Life took on a quality of unreality. Were these clothes really hers? Sobbing, all Sarah could do was collapse onto her bed. The same thoughts kept swirling in her head. Why couldn't I give Andi compassion when she needed it? Of course the boy was all wrong for her, but why did I have to let her see how glad I was when they broke up? Andi wrapped herself up in him, and when it was over, her whole teenage world fell apart, while I stood on the sidelines and applauded. Why the hell didn't I see it through her eyes? And now she's in the hands of strangers.

They decide what's best for her. How did we ever let this nightmare happen?

Sarah could not recall when or how she arrived in Dr. Zemmel's office. Seated by her husband in the waiting room, tense with fear, she could not prevent herself from inventing untold horrors. Sarah was so immersed in terror, she actually jumped at the psychiatrist's voice. "Hello, I'm Dr. Zemmel. Let's step into my office."

Sarah was gratified by his relaxed manner. He was certainly an improvement over her imagination. But Ed was immediately frantic, "What's going on Doctor? We've been trying to talk with someone about our daughter for two days, with no success. Now we're called into complete chaos. Bottom line, Doctor—what's wrong with Andi?"

"I'm going to be very candid with you," said Zemmel as he seated himself opposite Ed and Sarah. "We've been following a pretty standard routine and it's backfired. Obviously, she's had three fairly violent episodes in a short period of time which is extremely unusual."

Ed could barely contain himself. "Before you go any further, Dr. Zemmel, I'd like to know just how the hospital allowed Andi to endure three episodes. Isn't there any accountability here?"

"I realize your concern and I sympathize with you, Mr. Levy, which is why I called this meeting," replied Zemmel quietly. "Apparently we're dealing with a great deal of turbulence. Yet, I don't believe your daughter's lost touch with reality and that's a definite plus. Rather, she's distancing herself from her actions. In a sense, she's allowed herself to behave irrationally to relieve the tension."

"According to your theory, Andi is purposely being irrational," observed Ed. "I find that rather far fetched."

"Basically, I think she's acting out the hurt behind the anger," replied Zemmel very evenly.

"What hurt?" asked Sarah.

"That's what I'd like to talk to you about."

"Andi was very hurt when she and her boyfriend broke up. She was especially angry with me," said Sarah, "because Andi knew I never approved of the relationship in the first place."

"Why not?" asked Zemmel.

"Because the boy wasn't Jewish," intervened Ed testily. "I mentioned this to you earlier."

"Yes, you did, but I need more details to get a clearer picture," urged Zemmel.

"May I continue, Ed?" asked Sarah.

"Go on. I'm just on edge. Sorry."

"Andi knew I didn't approve all along and that never seemed to bother her. But when she realized how happy I was that Joe broke it off, she resented me terribly."

"So, it was the boy's idea to terminate the relationship," said Zemmel.

"It was," said Sarah quietly. "And I thought it was so convenient that I never even tried to help Andi with her grief. She hated me for not caring."

"Dr. Zemmel, may I go back to something you mentioned a few minutes ago?" asked Ed.

"Please, ask anything you'd like."

"You said Andi is behaving irrationally, but she hasn't really lost it."

"In a manner of speaking."

"What do you base that on? I don't mean to tell you how to run your therapy or whatever you call it, but Andi's behavior here sounds pretty off the wall to me. In fact, she's in worse shape since she entered the hospital than she was at home."

"Ed," exclaimed Sarah, "she tried to kill herself at home! What could be worse than that?"

"I meant up until that point," answered Ed tersely.

"Obviously, this is very difficult for both of you, but let's focus on right now," said Zemmel. "There is a pattern to Andi's behavior that is well thought out. I think it's clear that our conversation is providing some missing pieces to the puzzle. Most of your daughter's tantrums have centered around using the phone. She's obviously trying to get in touch with someone who's upsetting her. From Sarah's revelation, Andi's been involved in tumultuous relationships both inside and outside the family. Therefore, I believe her erratic behavior is being triggered by very real causes which are overwhelming her."

"Do you think she's trying to call her boyfriend?" asked Ed.

"It looks like a strong possibility," answered Zemmel.

"So what's your strategy, Doctor? How are you going to help my daughter? We seem to be talking in circles. Get to the point. It's only fair to tell you that I'm having real second thoughts about leaving Andi here."

"The point is that your daughter's been on a fairly heavy regimen of anti-psychotic medication, but she doesn't appear to be suffering from a psychosis. Rather, her symptoms are those of a panic disorder."

"Panic disorder!" screeched Ed and Sarah at once. The words were completely foreign to their vocabulary.

"I hope you're not just coming up with irrelevant theories to justify your position in this case," continued Ed. "It's true that my wife and I are not experts in psychiatry, but we're not idiots either. Basically, we're parents who want realistic help for our daughter."

"Actually, a panic disorder is a very well-documented syndrome," answered Zemmel.

"In case you don't know it, I'm an attorney, which means I must stay abreast of what's new in the world, and I don't mind telling you that I never heard of a panic disorder," Ed shot back.

"I'm somewhat surprised because panic disorders are fairly common, and the up side is that with a regimen of both medicine and therapy, they are very curable," responded Zemmel, hoping to placate his client.

"Now that you mention it, a friend of a friend's daughter was suffering from something I think they called a panic disorder," Sarah spoke almost to herself.

"Why are you so sure it's a panic disorder," asked Ed, who by now was secretly glad that Zemmel was finally offering hope.

"Panic disorders are marked by anxiety attacks that are often triggered by extreme stress. That explains much of Andi's behavior. In addition, I think she's been depressed for some time now."

"Do you think it's because of her relationship with Joe?" asked Sarah.

"Coupled by her relationship with you," answered Zemmel. "The important thing now is to create a completely non-stressful environment."

"But she's in a hospital already," noted Ed, "What more could she need?"

"I'm proposing 24-hour private duty care with no access to the telephone."

Sarah could barely mouth her next words, "Not even to call us? You can't possibly mean that."

"We must keep her environment as stable as possible, and free access to the phone could trigger another panic attack," Zemmel firmly maintained his position.

"Sarah," said Ed gently, finally warming toward Zemmel, "you said yourself that you and Andi aren't getting along too well at the moment."

"Andi's in a rough adolescent period," intervened Zemmel, grateful for Ed's support. "Her hormones are blasting and she's searching for expression. Once Andi begins therapy, along with proper medication, she'll learn to master the emotions she's struggling with. She'll discover the vocabulary and fortitude necessary for a dialogue that will lead to health."

"What kind of medication are you talking about?" asked Sarah, still skeptical. "The anti-psychotic drugs you prescribed seem to be turning her into a psychotic."

"As I said from the start, we were on the wrong track with the medication. Tomorrow I'm going to start her on Xanax and Pamelor. I'm hopeful that the results will be very positive."

"Try to stay calm, Sarah," said Ed. "Dr. Zemmel is trying to make some sense out of this nightmare, and, even though it's difficult, we've got to trust him."

"All this talk is driving me crazy," answered Sarah. "I want to trust, but all I can do is picture Andi scared and lonely. Please, can't we see her for just a few moments at least?"

"Would it be all right for us to have a short visit with Andi, just so we can see that she's all right?" Ed interjected.

Ed's eyes were even more pleading than his words, and Zemmel agreed to allow a brief visit. However, he was immediately interrupted by his beeper.

"Excuse me a moment."

"Shall we wait for you or can we go ahead and see Andi on our own?" asked Ed.

Zemmel was torn by the question. He knew he should accompany the Levys to see Andi, but he told himself no real harm would occur without him because the girl was so highly sedated. Yet, as he directed the Levys to Andi's floor, he suspected his true motivation. The beeper told him the call was from Bliss and he couldn't resist an irrepressible urge to call her immediately.

*　*　*　*

Seated on the edge of Andi's cot while she slept fitfully, Ed and Sarah couldn't stop looking at her. Her face was scratched and puffy. She also had a split upper lip and a blackened left eye. In addition, there were five stitches in her right shoulder. "How could this happen?" muttered Sarah. Both parents tried hard to see the girl they knew and loved underneath the cuts and bruises. Privately, they thanked G-d she was still alive.

"Look, she's getting up," whispered Ed to his wife.

Andi's eyes flickered open and gradually focused on her parents. She was very surprised to see them, and weakly extended her good arm to her mother.

"Mom, Dad," she whispered hoarsely, "you're here."

Her parents said little, unsure of how to respond. They were very grateful that Andi made contact with them, and the family relaxed in calm reunion.

Unfortunately, their quiet moment was quickly shattered by the clang of supper carts. Andi grew slightly nauseous from the smell of the food, but Sarah was immediately agitated. When she saw the tray placed on Andi's dresser, one of her nightmares solidified into reality.

"Ed," she said tensely "that food's not kosher!!"

"Didn't you order kosher food for her?" he whispered, trying not to disturb his daughter.

"Yes, but that's not it!"

"How do you know?"

When Sarah didn't answer him, Ed turned and his words instantly froze in his mouth. Andi, who previously could not even prop herself up, was now ramrod straight; her face ghastly white.

"Let me alone about kosher food," yelled Andi with all the strength she could muster. "I'll eat what I want, when I want, where I want." Ed wanted to comfort her, but felt powerless.

He sensed this was the turmoil Zemmel sought to circumvent, and attempted to inch his wife away. Wondering if Zemmel would return, Ed was stunned that Sarah wouldn't budge.

"Andi honey, please, we ordered you kosher food..."

Andi was adamant. "I'm having what I want to have. I'm sick of your damn rules."

Before Sarah could reply, she found herself staring into a rather strange but caring face.

"Hi, I'm Rose Schneider, your daughter's social worker. Maybe I can help you. What's the problem?"

Sarah assumed the woman was Jewish from her Israeli accent, and immediately confided, "We ordered kosher meals for her, but they're serving her the same as everyone else."

"Ma, leave me alone," Andi hissed from between clenched teeth.

Sarah whispered fiercely, through her tears, "We love you Andi. Why are you treating us like this?"

Persistent in her fight for self control, Andi contended, "It's not you, Ma. Don't you get it? This has to do with me. Ma, look at me! Don't you see where I am? Kosher food is important to you right now, not me. Stop trying to shove your shit down my throat!"

Ed desperately tried to move his wife out. He was disgusted with both Sarah and Andi, for putting him in an impossible position as usual. How dare Andi speak to her mother like that? Yet Sarah was also beyond his comprehension. Why wouldn't she stop? Zemmel said to keep Andi calm and that was sound advice. Besides, much of what Andi said made sense to him, even if he didn't like the way she put it. And who was this strange little woman tugging at Sarah's arm?

"Please, please Mrs. Levy, don't be so upset," begged Rose. "Maybe it doesn't have to be just black or white. Maybe there's a place for compromise."

"Look Miss," Ed bluntly asserted himself, "I don't mean to be rude, but confrontation is very bad for my daughter right now. So this whole discussion must be tabled before she has another panic attack. My wife and I really must leave for Andi's sake."

"But what about the food?" Sarah persisted.

"Look, Sar, stop with the food! Can't you see she's getting upset. We've got to get out!"

Andi watched the confusion from her corner and knew she didn't want her parents to go away feeling so hurt. But she desperately wanted them to respect her need to express herself. So she gathered her courage for a final try and she called out, "Ma!"

"Yes."

"I really don't hate you. But I've got to see things for myself...I'm sorry....Dad.."

"Yes, Baby.."

"Explain it to her, please."

His heart was splitting, when he promised. Just get better, he thought, and steered his wife to the door. Then he paused for a final glance at Andi. She half raised her arm, and waved at him from across the room.

"I love you, Baby," he mouthed silently as he fought an urge to run back to his daughter and hug her. Unaware of their contact, Sarah walked out the door.

CHAPTER 9

The next morning Andi awakened to the now-routine hospital morning sounds. She could barely lift her head. Inside and out, everything hurt; bruised body matched bruised psyche. She squinted at the sunlight that played on the floor, and propped herself on the pillow before she noticed the stranger seated on the chair by her bed. Andi decided to ignore him. She traced the sunlight from the floor to the window and brooded about her lack of freedom. But why this further invasion of privacy, she eventually asked herself, believing the youngish looking man seated next to her was there to spy.

"What are you doing here," she asked, despite herself.

"I'm available to go everywhere with you," he answered diplomatically.

"Even if I don't want you to?"

"You got it."

"Who wants this? My family?"

"Your doctor ordered 24-hour private nursing care for you."

"What? Why would he do that?"

"I think you may know the answer to that more than I do."

"So, you're here to protect me from myself."

"That's one way of looking at it."

"What other way is there?" she grumbled, secretly intrigued.

"I'm here to help you cope with your emotions."

"Right now, I just want to go to the bathroom. Can't I go alone?"

"Nope, you have to buy back your freedom in this place."

Andi knew she wasn't strong enough to get to the bathroom alone, but she still resented losing her privacy. Continual guard by a complete stranger fueled her anguish.

"I hate this place. They're always trapping me, always on top of me. They make my feelings come out and then just ask for more."

"Calm down, Andi. That's why I'm here. You need to relax. We can talk about how you feel on the inside, so maybe some of your intensity will be decreased."

Admittedly engrossed, Andi wasn't fully convinced. "What about my privacy?"

"You're right. This place is short on privacy. Instead, sharing is emphasized here. We talk about things held in for too long."

"Hey, how come you know so much?"

"I've been where you are. I know what it's like. It's easy falling in, but hard climbing out."

"I'll never get out."

"You will, but it's a long curvy road."

"What's your name?" asked Andi as the nurse helped her to her feet and they started to slowly walk toward the lavatories.

"Danny."

"Do you know Dr. Zemmel?"

"Sure. He's pretty laid back, but don't be fooled. He's tough."

"He does something that makes me mad."

"What?"

"He purposely doesn't talk to me a lot. He just sits there and stares. It really drives me up the wall." They reached the bathrooms and she hesitated as usual. "I hate these toilets."

"Go on in," he urged. "I'll be right here waiting."

Once inside, she saw Tina at the sinks. Andi was too embarrassed to talk and quickly entered a stall. But Tina's persistence was difficult to evade.

"I notice you have a shadow this morning."

"Ummm," Andi wished the girl would leave her alone.

"So did I."

Andi was caught in a web of curiosity. "How was it?"

"At first it seemed that nothing belonged to just me anymore. I was forced to share everything and I hated it. A real invasion of privacy."

Andi was unnerved, as she listened to this girl who looked and spoke like she belonged in an Honors English class, rather than a mental institution. But sounds of flushing toilets quickly drew Andi from her reverie. "What finally happened?" she asked.

"After I got over wanting to disintegrate, I learned to share...everything. That's the way we live in here. The whole staff hits you in the place most of the world tries to ignore."

"You mean they focus on the ugly part?"

"Yeah, answered Tina very quietly. "And it's gruesome to look at what you see as unattractive. Except they try to make you see you're really attractive after all. They work on new interpretations. It's called reframing."

"So that's what therapy's about," whispered Andi to herself, as she walked to the sink and was dismayed to find only cold water.

"I gotta go now. I'm late to class," called Tina as she walked away. Let's talk later."

Andi tried to work up a lather of soap despite the cold water and glimpsed some pride in herself. This place was definitely rock bottom, but she wasn't disintegrating. In fact, as she noticed the slash marks on her wrists, she was thankful she didn't die that awful night. Back then, she couldn't see anything beyond her desolation. But maybe there were new things to learn that she never thought existed. Tina exuded a mystery that Andi wanted to both uncover and avoid. For the first time in quite a while, Andi glimpsed the promise that life held. Even her jailer didn't appear so alarming, as she walked towards him.

"By the way, you start school this morning right after you see your shrink," said Danny in greeting.

Thoughts of school triggered memories of Joe. She pictured him in classes with her vacant seat staring at everyone. Once more passion rose inside, and she couldn't bear his refusal to return her feeling. He must care. She was sure that if she truly revealed her love for him, he would admit his own. Despite his

48

rejection, she would call him again, Andi decided fiercely. "Do I have time for a quick phone call," she asked Danny in a voice she hoped sounded normal.

Opting for distraction rather than direct confrontation, the nurse changed the subject. Danny was so skillful that Andi soon found herself in Zemmel's office without once recognizing his manipulation.

"Good morning, Andi," began Zemmel in upbeat tones.

"Ummmph."

Building on the rapport they were developing in the last session, Zemmel attempted engaging her once more.

"How are you today?"

When he saw Andi wasn't responsive, Zemmel maintained silence. As usual, Andi was more susceptible to his silence than his words.

"What do you want me to say," she whined.

"Whatever comes to mind."

"I'm mad at you."

"Talk more about being mad."

"Why did you send that guy? He goes everywhere I go. You treat me like a baby."

"I don't think you really want to be alone right now."

"Oh, you don't? How do you know what I want? Besides, I don't have any privacy."

"Andi, I believe the last thing you actually want is privacy."

"Why?"

"Every time you lost control, you were reaching out from loneliness. You were fighting the terror inside. Danny is not some stranger. He's a registered psychiatric nurse who will be there for you in the empty moments, when sharing is important."

"So, he's there to keep me from going crazy. I knew it all along."

"Tell me your thoughts on going crazy."

"You're trying to trick me. You're trying to make me crazy with your questions."

"No one can make you crazy, Andi. But I sense you fear it."

"You think I'm afraid I'm crazy."

"Are you?"

Andi shielded her eyes from his gaze and whispered, "I must be crazy or I wouldn't act like this."

"Andi," Zemmel spoke carefully, "talk to me about why you acted out yesterday."

"When situations look hopeless, I get crazy. I can't stand weakness in myself and I want to destroy the obstacles. So I start to push away anything that stands in my way."

"What stood in your way that caused you to become so angry after lunch?"

"I called Joe, but he wouldn't talk to me. He was my only hope, and when that was gone I had nothing. I couldn't breathe. I couldn't think. All I could do was knock at a wall inside myself. Then everything went numb and all the pain was gone. For one moment, I was strong and powerful."

"So, it's frustration that fires your anxiety," mused Zemmel.

Andi bit her fingers to keep from screaming and hated herself for having opened up. Their talk made her feel completely unprotected from the forces she tried to avoid. She made herself look past the stuffy office and dark green hospital shades and pictured Joe. His eyes were warm and smiling. She was sure he was the one that could save her from this nightmare, if she could only convince him of her love.

Out loud she said, "I need to make a phone call."

Zemmel coughed and mentally fortified himself for the onslaught he foresaw, "Right now the phone is off limits."

"What? How can that be? I just used it yesterday."

"That's very true," said Zemmel, speaking as flatly as possible. "But for now we're trying to keep life peaceful. We don't want any outside disruption that might upset you."

"We? Who's we? Nobody asked me anything. Nobody cares about what I think." Pausing, she grimaced, "Oh, I know. It's my parents. You're with them." Angrily spitting her words by now, Andi shrilled, "I get it. You don't care about me. This is all a hoax to do their bidding. And I thought I could trust you. Hah, what an idiot I was!"

"Look Andi, I'm sorry if I didn't state things clearly, but the decision was mine alone. When I said `we', I meant that I discussed it with your parents, and they agreed. I didn't mean to imply it was their idea. It certainly wasn't."

Andi was unwilling to accept what she had just heard, and rebelled against the notion of putting feelings into words. Words could no longer convey the anger coursing through her. Emotions screamed for action and she reached for whatever she could grasp. She grabbed a book from the bookcase adjacent to her and hurled it across the room at Zemmel's feet. Punctuating her action with words, she screamed at the top of her lungs, "I hate you, asshole. I'm not going to let you run my life."

Calmly sucking on his cough drop, Zemmel attempted to close the session.

"You're angry with me and that's something we can talk about tomorrow."

"Tomorrow, bullshit! I want to call Joe today."

"I'm sorry Andi, but it's a judgment I have to make. For now, there are no phone calls."

"You see me," she said raising her good arm angrily, "I'm going to throw the whole shelf at you."

"I don't think so."

"Why not?" she asked, arm poised.

"Because you're talking about it, rather than doing it. That's the point of therapy; putting thought and feeling into words to heal the hurt and frustration inside."

"It cuts like a knife," she whispered in her soft voice, allowing her arm to fall.

"I know, but we're facing your pain together."

"I still want to call Joe. Only he can take away my hurt."

"We don't know that," said Zemmel in his gentlest voice. Andi could not bear to hear that Joe might not be there for her anymore, and collapsed into a fit of tears. Zemmel decided to extend the therapy a few extra minutes because he understood the importance of her tears. He sensed a turning point. Andi was very weak, but there was honesty in her tears. Through them, he was certain she would find a voice that was truly her own.

CHAPTER 10

Andi left her session reeling. Inwardly focused, she saw no one. Danny said little as he led her from the psychiatrist's office to her cot. He recognized her extreme vulnerability and understood that she wasn't ready to talk. After he allowed Andi to rest briefly, Danny led his zombie-like charge down a long corridor.

Andi was aware that Danny deposited her in a chair by a desk, and left. When she furtively peeked through her fingers to explore, all she saw was a room with a high ceiling and sick green walls that were as nondescript as the rest of the floor. But then she spotted the bright curtains on the windows and the travel posters hiding plaster spots. She caught a cheerful undercurrent and observed the circular pattern of the desks. Everyone faced each other. As usual, there was no privacy—no room for escape. This must be the classroom, she thought.

Sandi Glover sat at the mouth of the circle. She was the teacher. A 58 year old heavyset black woman, previously a public high school teacher and principal, and very involved in her church, Sandi believed her calling was in alternative education. As a teacher in the hospital, she achieved fulfillment that eluded her elsewhere. She was able to speak to the inner ear of her students, and she often became the mainstay of the young people in her class.

Ms. Glover, as her students called her, understood how much a kid could hurt, and so she encouraged self expression in all their activities. Her aura of tough warmth gave an earthy quality to her classroom, and inspired ease in those who were often stifled by other settings. Though new students usually tried to hide what hurt them, Ms. Glover never permitted them to pretend pain wasn't there. No one was humiliated or shamed for carrying a burden of hurt. Instead, all were encouraged to open and share.

"We're all here to heal," Ms. Glover often advised, "and you'll never heal by hiding your wounds." Kids so often shattered by mockery suffered on the outside, would take their time trusting her. But having gained their trust, she never lost it.

At the back of the classroom was a wish chart where kids drew pictures of their hopes—dreams often abandoned after years of loneliness and misunderstanding in the brutal onslaught of mental illness. She encouraged students to nurture their rediscovered dreams, so they could use them as a bridge to a whole life.

"Never let go," Ms. Glover told her kids; "when it gets dark, don't give in. Don't give up. Reach out, reach up and hang on. Hang on to that dream. It's your right. Never let it go."

Stars bearing the names of the students were pasted on the chart. "You are tomorrow's stars," Ms. Glover often told the class, pointing to the stars, "and don't forget it. You are the future, each and every one of you. You are important to the world. Just because you're here doesn't mean you're finished. You will heal and take your place in the world. And you'll shine. Remember, everyone here is a shining star."

The class was in the middle of a math lesson, when Andi entered. Ms. Glover stopped work to welcome her to the group. When Andi didn't respond, Ms. Glover let her know it was all right. "We'll be here for you when you're ready to join us in spirit as well as body," she said and went into the back closet to get some extra supplies for her.

Tina was very glad to see Andi, even if she looked less than composed. Except for Tina and Andi, all were boys. It was horrible being the only girl with three boys. Tina hoped Andi was more in touch than she appeared and immediately tried to make contact.

"Andi," she called, "come sit by me."

Andi wanted to get up. She wanted to be next to Tina, but she couldn't move. Her legs felt leaden. Tina couldn't understand what was wrong and tried again. "Andi, I thought we were going to be friends."

"Friends," shot back a boy from the class, named Tony. "Who'd wanna be your friend?"

"Shut up, freak," snapped Tina, who once again looked to Andi for a response. But Andi still could not collect herself enough to say anything.

By now, Tony was out of his seat waving his hand in front of Andi. "Look," he shrieked, "she doesn't move. We've got a real live zombie." And with that, he began jumping up and down in front of Andi in an imitation of an ape.

Andi couldn't believe her eyes. What do you want from me, she tried to shriek at the top of her lungs. But it was as if her lips were paralyzed. Nothing moved. Oh my G-d, she thought. I'm gonna have another fit. Please, please G-d. Don't let it happen. Not in front of these imbeciles.

Fortunately, Tina spoke for her. "Ms. Glover," she yelled, "they're going crazy on the new girl."

"Why shouldn't we go crazy?" retorted Tony, "Aren't we insane?"

Ms. Glover came back carrying some books and paper for Andi just as Tina was about to deck Tony, who was a foot shorter than she was. But the teacher didn't lose her cool. "I heard that about being crazy, and as far as I'm concerned, crazy is a word that's lost it's meaning. Everyone has space for self-expression here as long as it doesn't interfere with anyone else. Now, what seems to be the problem?" she asked, as everyone sat down.

"Tony was invading the new girl's space," offered Carlos in his usual soft spoken manner.

"I was just trying to see if she was alive," countered Tony. "Tina was the one bothering her."

"I was just asking Andi to sit next to me," explained Tina.

"Is that so, Miss Bossiness?" asked Tony sarcastically.

"That's enough of that," interceded Ms. Glover. And then she turned to Andi who was peeping at the action through her fingers. "Would you like to sit next to Tina?"

Once more Andi found herself the focus of attention. But this time, she was more relaxed. She realized that she didn't throw a fit when they were making fun of her. She hadn't made a fool of herself after all. It was like she was getting a second chance to be normal and she took it. Her voice was low, but charged with feeling. "Yes," she said, and easily moved to the spot next to Tina.

"And now," said Ms. Glover, as she handed Andi her supplies, "back to math."

"Must we?" whined Tina.

"Why not?" said Carlos, who always tried to be positive, "I like it."

"Me too," chimed in Andi very unexpectedly.

"The mummy has spoken," chirped Tony. But his taunt was more of an acceptance than an insult, and it didn't seem to bother Andi, so Ms. Glover let it pass.

Instead, she was happy to see that the kids were interrelating fairly well, and smiled inwardly at their success. Tony was right, she thought. Andi did look like the walking dead when she came in. It's a miracle that she's participating at all. But she was jarred from her reverie by a young man who rarely spoke. Now he was rocking back and forth in his chair, and stabbing his pencil into the paper.

"Relax Jerry," coaxed Ms. Glover. "Don't let these word problems get the best of you."

"Humph," Jerry finally spoke, "I hate them."

"Try to remember what you just read."

Reality was always fading in and out so rapidly for Jerry, it was difficult for him to keep track of it; word problems were especially frustrating. "You know it's hard for me to remember," he finally answered.

"I know, but I want you to try."

"Like the new girl tried?"

"Exactly Jerry. That's it."

"Maybe I can help you," offered Carlos.

"Why, that would be great, Carlos," exclaimed Ms. Glover. It's amazing what these kids can do, she reflected, as Carlos went over to help Jerry. They're so lost and lonely when they first arrive here. They're overwhelmed by all kinds of ugliness. It seems like their inner beauty is forever lost. Yet it's really there, just waiting for eyes human enough to see it.

CHAPTER 11

"Aaaghowwa!" The floor filled with incredible noise, "Get off me, motherfucker! Get off my back. Don't you dare touch me. Don't come near me." Yolanda Smith, a 15-year-old girl weighing at least 200 pounds was scared and bloody. She refused to let anyone properly dress the wounds on her face and upper body. Her clothes were torn and she was wildly angry. "Get your white hands off me. I got my rights," she yelled at anyone who came near.

* * * *

Madi had just settled down for a private smoke in an obscure corner of the floor when she noticed the emergency light blinking and heard the screams. She didn't move. All she could visualize was extra work. Why are all the emergencies coming here these days, she complained to herself. I bet it's another one of those kids who really belongs in Irvington General, but all their beds are filled. This mess just never ends. Let someone else take care of it, she thought, as she saw people running around trying to get the new girl into an empty bed.

The night shift tended to make Madi introspective. While she smoked, she remembered her first years at the hospital. Then, each case was a challenge; someone to help, a human being who needed her. She used to love going to work.

Right from the start, she knew it was more than just the money. She actually loved psychiatric nursing. Very attuned to the inmates, she sympathized with the needs and hurts that often drove friends and relatives away. She reached into hearts virtually stunted by illness and, very often, the patients reached back into hers. Indeed, some of those bonds were even deeper than the ones she formed with her own family. On those days that she was forced to stay home because one of her children was sick, she actually missed the hospital.

But enthusiasm died. Madi now threw each day into the trash like an old newspaper, often unread and definitely unwanted. She was unable to recall the particular days or events that led to her disillusionment. Rather, it was an accumulation of many daily annoyances with administration, bureaucracy, doctors, and feeling unimportant. Perhaps it was just too many years in the same place.

Madi never actually concluded exactly what it was, but one morning she decided she was tired. Staying in bed an extra hour was more important than the old ties to the hospital. Sometimes she tried fooling herself into believing the patients were different. However, in lucid moments like this one, she clearly saw the difference was in herself.

*   *   *   *

Andi stared at the new patient who was finally placed in the empty cot diagonally across the room, and recalled the blood and rage of her own drama. As she reentered the nightmare of her last month at home, she pictured her mother in the kitchen having coffee with a friend. They always discussed their children privately, but this time Andi overheard her mother's voice, "Thank G-d it's over. He was never right for her. He wasn't Jewish. She rebelled and now it's finished. It was just a phase. Thank G-d, she can forget about him and get on with her life."

Andi's frustration mounted with her mother's words. They were so unfair. They left no room for Andi to think for herself. The bitterness of the moment overpowered her and she rushed into the kitchen where her mother sat talking with her friend.

"All I want is to be like other kids; go where I want, with whom I want, when I want. But you don't see it that way, do you?" screeched Andi to the chagrin of her mother's friend. "No,

Mom. You want to make all the decisions. You want to keep all the control."

And then her father, disturbed from reading his paper, sent Andi to her room. But even as Andi climbed the stairs to her room, her mother couldn't resist a final comment.

"We never stopped you Andi," she said. "You know that. But now that it's over, I'm glad."

"I know you're glad," sobbed Andi. "I suppose you're glad that everything that's important to me means absolutely nothing to you."

"Andi, please," countered her mother, "you know I didn't mean it that way."

"Go to your room, Andi," came her father's voice once more. "We'll talk about this later after you're calm."

But Andi couldn't squelch her anger, "No, Mom. You meant exactly what you said. And you're right. It's finished. My life's finished. I have nothing left. I gave it all away to Joe, and he flushed it down the toilet. Don't you understand. It wasn't just a rebellion. It was my life. And that's gone, done, ended. It was my life and I lost it. I let it get away from me." Andi was finally in her room and she threw herself on the bed. "Ma," she wept into her pillow, "don't you see that? Don't you see me?"

Andi didn't want to remember anymore and instinctively called for Danny, but there was no response. I'm alone, she realized, not quite sure how she felt about it. But the new girl held her interest and she sat up on her cot for a better look. What brought her here? Was she really nuts? Did she also want to die?

Almost against her will, Andi continued to use the girl as a mirror to recall the events of her own horror the night she was put in the hospital. She remembered the way her friend Cathy telephoned to let her know Joe was at the movies with someone else. Andi believed Joe when he suggested they separate for a few days just to think things over. He never hinted at someone else and Andi never even considered the possibility. Cathy's words put a knife into her heart that cut deeper than the blade she eventually used on herself. There was nothing left without the hope of a relationship with Joe. She took her friend's words as proof of Joe's complete betrayal and went numb. All the air was sucked out of her lungs. There was no oxygen—everything appeared dreamlike and distant. Even her anger with her mother lost its importance.

At the time, she noticed that life didn't hurt so much when you decided that nothing really mattered. The situation grew overwhelmingly hopeless, while she diminished. Only her pounding heartbeat was large. It felt like someone else's fingers gathered the strength to hold the blade that finally slashed into her flesh. She actually experienced little pain from her father's razor blade, but from across a great void she noticed a swelling redness of dripping blood that was staining her wrists. And then there was the hospital.

"Hi there."

Andi was so transported into her reverie that she jumped at the sound of Tina's voice.

"I heard there was a lot of action in these parts," continued Tina in a confidential whisper.

"Yeah, it's a real hot night," Andi propelled herself back to the present, "It kind of reminded me..."

"Of yourself," interjected Tina.

"Yeah."

"I know. Guess we've all been there. That's why we're here."

"Tina, you make it sound so simple. But when I start thinking about things, I get so mad and helpless, I stop functioning."

"Ever try writing?"

"What d'ya mean?"

"Writing a journal. Every day I record what I think, feel, fantasize about; stuff like that."

"No, I don't want to write about it. I want to do it."

"Do what?"

"You know, things..."

"Like?"

"Like be with my damn boyfriend. Only problem is, he's rotten. He doesn't want to be with me."

Suddenly, an electric current went through Tina. "Listen Andi, I knew there was something I meant to tell you."

Andi tensed when she realized they were about to have a major discussion, but she motioned Tina to continue.

"You know how I work in the nurse's station," began Tina.

"No, but go on."

"Well, I heard them talking."

"About what?"

"About you."

"Me?" exclaimed Andi, not quite sure how she should react.

"Yeah. They were saying how someone's calling you...some guy. And your shrink doesn't want you to know."

Andi paled visibly.

"Oh shit," muttered Tina, scared by Andi's reaction. Even the new girl grew quiet.

Tina continued to stare at her friend until she noticed Andi turn blue. "My G-d," yelled Tina, "she's gonna die."

Madi was just finishing her private smoke when she again heard commotion in the A wing. This time she knew she couldn't avoid it. "Damn," she cursed, as she stubbed out the cigarette with her shoe. "It must be that new one they put near Andi Levy."

But when Madi went to Yolanda's cot, her jaw dropped. The 200-pound girl was calmly staring at the ceiling.

"Wha...what's going on here?" Madi sputtered uncertainly.

Yolanda slowly comprehended that she was the only coherent one there, and casually pointed to Andi. "That girl ain't breathin'."

"It's...it's all my fault," choked Tina. "I told her."

"Told her what?" asked Madi and turned to face Tina.

"About the phone calls."

Madi quickly assembled the pieces and recalled a young man's insistent voice asking for Andi Levy. She also recognized the signs of a panic attack in Andi and immediately sought to calm her, so that she would start breathing.

"Hang in there! Breathe deep. That's the girl. Come on, let's do that again; in and out. That's right. That's good."

Slowly, Andi responded and her color came back while quiet tears streamed down her face. Madi decided there was no need for extra medication.

"Andi, let's talk," suggested Madi. "What happened here tonight?"

Andi immediately began stammering, "Dr. Zemmel, he..."

"What about Dr. Zemmel?"

Andi threw herself face down on the cot in silent hysteria and refused to talk. Remembering that Zemmel was working late that night, Madi beeped him. Let him handle this, she told herself and turned to Andi once more.

"O.K., hon. Doctor will be here very soon."

"I don't want to see him."

"Just relax. We'll work it all out. You'll see. But for now, just calm down."

"So this is why they call it the nut house," observed the newcomer to no one in particular. "Everybody sure buggin' out tonight."

"What's your name?" called Tina from Andi's cot.

"Yolanda Smith, but everybody calls me Bubba."

"Why Bubba?"

"Cause when I was little I loved to blow bubbles, but instead of saying `bubbles' I said `bubbas'. So they called me Bubba."

Yolanda was surprised to see a bearded man in a business suit carrying a briefcase. "Who's he?" she asked Tina.

"Oh, that's Dr. Zemmel, Andi's psychiatrist.

"Wooh, I thought he was comin' for me. They goin' to give me one of them?"

"In this place, we all get shrinks. That's what we do here," answered Tina.

"That's what you do here. I'm gettin' out in the morning."

Zemmel walked over to Andi's cot and sat on the chair. "Hi, Andi," he opened the impromptu session. Upon getting no answer, he continued. "I see you're upset, but I'm glad you're keeping control."

"Go away."

Sitting quietly next to Andi, Zemmel waited for more. As usual, his instincts were correct.

"I trusted you."

Zemmel remained silent.

"Do you hear me?"

"I hear you."

"So say something."

"What I have to say isn't important. This is your therapy and your thoughts are what count."

"You double crossed me. I hate you! You just work for them."

"Are you talking about your parents?"

"Obviously, I'm talking about my parents. I thought you were on my side, but you're on theirs. I hate you!"

"So you believe I betrayed you, Andi."

"Yeah, you betrayed me. Now we both know, so you can leave."

Again, he gave no response.

Andi, sobbing by now, barely choked out her words. "You know I love him and want to hear from him, but you won't let me call him. And now, you won't even let me take his calls."

"Andi," said Zemmel, moved by the girl's pleading, "if he cares for you, he'll wait. You know that."

"I don't know that."

"Yes you do. Actually, I think you're concerned about whether or not you can trust me."

"You're right, I don't trust you. I thought you understood my love for Joe, but you don't!"

"I think Joe betrayed your feelings for him, and now you're afraid I will do the same thing."

"Don't compare yourself to Joe," screamed Andi. "You're always trying to mix me up. Joe's the one I want to talk to—not you! Why the hell won't you let me talk to him? Are you jealous or something?"

Zemmel flushed inwardly at her uncanny perception. He was envious of her ability to sustain intense feelings. Wasn't that a good part of his attraction for Bliss? But he maintained his usual outward poise.

"I don't want you taking Joe's calls for the same reason I don't want you talking to anyone on the outside," Zemmel answered quietly. "You've suffered a severe trauma that landed you in the hospital. Now our job is to work through all those vulnerable feelings and find what it takes to make Andi feel good inside. As I said before, if Joe really likes you, he'll wait. Otherwise, we'll talk about it."

"Why should he wait? You just said he betrayed my feelings. You don't think he really cares for me."

"When I said he betrayed your feelings, I meant that he hurt you. He let you down. People often hurt each other in the course of a relationship. That doesn't always mean that they don't care. But when people do care, they are usually willing to wait."

Andi really liked the way Zemmel took time to explain things. She turned around and actually smiled. "You always make me like you even though I hate you."

"That makes as much sense as anything else around here," commented Yolanda eavesdropping.

"But please, can't I just have one tiny phone call to him?" persisted Andi.

"Andi, let's not beat a dead horse. It's late and you need to get some sleep. For that matter, so do I," he said lightly, and then remembered he wasn't going home.

Andi said nothing. In her imagination, she was already forging a new relationship with her old boyfriend. He called and that's all that really mattered. She reached out for feelings she couldn't forget, and embraced Joe in her mind.

Zemmel was aware of the gleam in his patient's eyes and knew keeping the situation stable would be challenging. She was tough, but that fascinated him. It would certainly be a test of his own strength to bring Andi's cauldron of feelings into her therapy. Well, he thought, blandly popping an omnipresent cough drop—to be continued.

Back at her station, Madi remembered Danny was missing. He wasn't with the Levy girl. Where was he? Danny was great with kids, which was why Zemmel put him on Andi's case. But his personal problems overwhelmed him at times and then there was trouble. Madi knew what her position demanded, and immediately went to the supply closet to see if any drugs were missing. She was startled by a movement in the shadows, but wasn't surprised to see that it was Danny.

"Danny," called Madi in a harsh whisper, "what are you doing here?" He approached her sheepishly. "Where were you?" she demanded. "That kid almost went off. I beeped Zemmel."

Danny didn't answer, but taking one look at his eyes, Madi knew the truth. Her worst fears concerning him were confirmed.

"Oh G-d Danny, I thought you were over all that. Plus, look what you're doing to me. You know I'm responsible for the drug check."

"Madi, please help me. It's been rough at home lately and I lost my head. You know you're the only one I can count on."

Danny was like a kid brother to Madi. She always did what she could for him, but now she knew he was clearly abusing drugs and all she could feel was drained. Almost in relief, she remembered Zemmel.

"I really don't know what you expect me to do Danny," she attempted to placate him, "and anyway, there's Zemmel. He's got to know you weren't with the patient."

"Tell him I was on an emergency. Tell him my dog was sick. Tell him anything. I'm desperate. Can't you understand?"

"You're forgetting something Danny! What about the missing pills? How can I account for them?"

"Say you gave them to the kid. Tell him she was freaking and needed medication."

Madi opened her mouth to speak, but wasn't quite sure what to say, when she thankfully noticed Zemmel walking towards them. "Danny, don't look now, but he's coming," she whispered.

"Who?" he whispered back, too high and caught up in his problems to fully absorb the situation.

"Who do you think? Zemmel, of course."

"Are you with me?"

"I...I Danny, I honestly don't know what to say. Of course I want to help you, but..."

Madi relaxed when Zemmel interrupted, "Danny, we have to talk."

"Look, Doctor...I can explain." He paused and looked toward Madi, who purposely looked away.

Zemmel quickly sized up the situation and asked Danny to meet him in his office. "We have to sort things out. I'll be there in a moment," he told Danny.

"When is Mary's shift?" Zemmel asked Madi once Danny was out of earshot.

"A.M." responded Madi quickly, hoping there would be no more questions.

"O.K., put her on the Levy case. Danny is off, temporarily at least."

"What about right now?"

"For now, Andi's resting. Our talk was productive. I'm sure she'll keep till morning. Good night, Madi."

"Good night, Dr. Zemmel," said Madi, as politely as possible. Relieved that she wasn't asked to betray her friend, Madi searched for a match and took her first forbidden puff. Zemmel was one of the better ones, but her respect for him was guarded. She prayed he was right about Andi Levy, because in her opinion the girl should not be left alone for five minutes.

Andi was unaware of the politics swirling around her, and sorted things at her own pace. She decided she liked Zemmel and the way he approached her problems. He wasn't as intense about things as her parents were. He didn't expect her to solve problems at his convenience. There was no pressure in therapy when she couldn't find the right words. She talked to him about things she never dared even think about before. She trusted him to give her time and space to put her own thoughts together, rather than forcing her to accept his. They didn't always agree, but he always listened. She sensed his faith in her; his belief that she was capable of growing strong and healthy.

But at the same time, she brooded about Zemmel's rules, especially where they concerned Joe. She told herself that her boyfriend was none of Dr. Zemmel's business, and began scheming about her love life. At first, the situation appeared completely hopeless. There was always somebody watching and the phone was off limits. Then just as the old frustration besieged her, new strength intervened and she knew she could solve her problem. There definitely was a solution and she would surely find it.

Glad that she wasn't panicking, Andi remembered Danny wasn't there. I'm free, she realized. No one's watching me. I'll do it. I'll call Joe right now. But reaching for her change, she recalled it was spent. Gradually, Andi felt eyes from across the room.

"Hey, it's really dull here," called Yolanda when she saw Andi's head turn in her direction. "I wanna talk. They call me Bubba. What's your name?

"Andi."

"Why you here?"

"Long story."

"I got time," persisted Yolanda.

"Why you here?" asked Andi, trying to change the subject.

"Fighting."

Seeing Andi's surprise, Yolanda continued. "I really don't belong here. Irvington General was all filled up, so they just brought me here to kinda cool down."

"Is that why you were yelling so much?"

"Mostly. So why you here?"

"I tried to kill myself," said Andi quietly, surprised to hear herself talking about this to anyone. "See that blood above your cot?"

"Yeah."

"I'm always scared it's mine. Most of the time I try not to look at it. What were your fighting about?" Andi asked after a pause.

Yolanda laughed aloud and felt more like herself. "What else? Love!"

"That's funny! That's why I wanted to kill myself. It was because of love. At least that's what I thought it was."

"You'll never catch me killin' myself over that. Maybe somebody else, but not me."

"But lately, I'm not so sure about love anymore."

"Why not?"

"I used to think that if I got everything I wanted like clothes and stuff, it meant my parents loved me. And I always begged them for lots of things. But now I don't think love works that way. After bein' in here, I don't know how it works."

Boy does she sound brainwashed, thought Yolanda and tried to change the subject to something more interesting. "So, how'd you try to kill yourself?"

"I know I slit my wrists and then it's a blank. I barely remember how I got here."

"Wooh, I sure remember how I got here," exclaimed Yolanda. It was a real trip."

"I sort of remember being bandaged," continued Andi. "It was like being dead and waking up. All I could hear were the lyrics to this song."

"What was the song?"

Andi's mouth opened and then shut automatically. Reminiscing put her where she was afraid to go. She preferred things to be vague lately. Maybe the blood on the ceiling was hers; maybe it wasn't. Maybe it didn't matter.

"Hey, you still with us?"

"I'm…I'm not sure; can't really talk about it." Andi turned to her wall, the only protection she could count on and fell asleep.

*　　*　　*　　*

There was a hand on Andi's breast. In her sleep, she tried to brush it away, but it remained there.

"Joe, is that you?" she asked in semi-fog.

"Yeah, yeah it's Joe. Now shut up," came a rough voice.

Andi started to shake off grogginess.

"You're not Joe, you're…"

A hand was clapped over her mouth. "Shut up."

Fingers started working their way down her body, underneath her gown. Andi fought for alertness. When the choking feeling came, she mastered it, drew all her strength together and kicked the form above her in the groin. She unbalanced him! He stumbled and ran!

When she opened her mouth to scream, no sound came forth. Who will believe me? They'll say I'm nuts! They'll give me two guards instead of one, she told herself. But I know it was Danny! That was his voice!

This was a new terror for Andi. Her body stiffened. She thought about his hands. Helplessness terrified her. What if he shows up again? What if he's here in the morning? He's my nurse, she almost screamed out loud, and then gagged at the thought of his face—her mouth dry with fear. She still sensed his fingers. She felt their coldness on her breast. Whatever they touched was dirty. I've got to tell, screeched a voice from inside.

You can't! You're a mental patient! Who will believe you? They'll say you're fantasizing—and maybe you are!

I wasn't, she screamed back at herself. I saw him. I heard his voice and I still feel his ugly fat hands all over me.

There were footsteps. Andi cowered, afraid to move.

"Oh Andi, you're up," said Madi. "Dr. Zemmel said to give you this." As the nurse extended the pill and a cup of water, Andi wanted to scream out what just happened. She wanted arms around her. She craved a soft voice assuring her that she was safe. She needed someone to say they'd catch him and throw him in jail. But she told herself it wouldn't happen that way and just swallowed the pill.

"You look tense," commented Madi. "Try and get some sleep."

I want to talk, Andi almost screamed. Shut up came a command from somewhere in her head. "Where's Danny?" she finally blurted.

Madi looked at the girl, unsure of what to say. "Why do you ask?"

"I thought I'm supposed to have someone with me all the time," replied Andi with surprising composure.

"Danny's having some personal problems and won't be in tonight."

"What about in the morning?"

The question unsettled Madi. She didn't quite know how to respond. How much could she tell? Well, Andi would find out soon enough, she reasoned, so why not let her know now?

"I don't know if I'm supposed to tell you this, but Dr. Zemmel took Danny off your case."

Relief zoomed through Andi. I'm safe from him, the told herself. But what about tonight? What if he comes back tonight? Tell, she screamed inwardly. Someone's got to believe me. He must be in trouble anyway. Why else would Dr. Zemmel get rid of him? Maybe they'll send the cops!

Hah! No matter what his problems are, you're still the patient. They'll never believe you, she answered herself.

The medicine took effect before Andi could think of more alternatives. Madi wondered why the girl looked so relieved when she heard Danny wouldn't be there in the morning. Most kids liked him. But she decided to remain uninvolved. Satisfied that Andi was asleep, she left.

CHAPTER 12

"I want outta here," boomed Yolanda. "I don't need to be in no nut house. They just brought me here 'cause Irvington General was full."

"Please Yolanda," pleaded the social worker, Rose Schneider.

"Don't call me Yolanda. Nobody does; not even my mother."

"Well, what do you want me to call you?"

Beginning to laugh, all 200 pounds of the girl shook.

"You sure got a strange way of talkin', lady."

"You mean my accent?" questioned Rose with spunk.

"Is that what you call it? Yeah, I guess that's what I'm talkin' about."

"So what do you want me to call you?" asked Rose impatiently.

"Lady, like I told you, I don't want you to call me nothing. I just wanna get outta here."

Rose tried a new tack, and made her voice as authoritative as possible. "Look, we're not going to get anywhere like this."

Sensing the resolution of the bird-like woman before her, Yolanda relented. "Call me Bubba."

"O.K. Bubba, take a look at yourself. You can't go anywhere in this condition. Your wounds must heal first."

"But I don't like this place," resisted Yolanda.

"Many don't like it at first, but they learn to get along. We're going to try to help you manage your life more effectively, so you don't fight so much. Perhaps you'll learn to channel your energy in more positive directions.

Caught off guard, Yolanda's voice started booming again. "Channel my energy? Lady, I don't mean no disrespect. I know you're tryin' to help me, but your talkin' a mess of crazy stuff."

Loud voices woke up Andi and she remembered Danny immediately. She wanted to disappear. Another day of him was unthinkable.

"Hi there, good to see you up," said Mary brightly.

New company, observed Andi to herself. Who's this one? Another psychopath? At least it's not Danny.

Mary didn't wait for a response and continued. "Danny's not going to be around for a while, Andi. So it's just us right now."

The nurse's congenial tone only served to increase Andi's distrust. But Andi was glad she made it through the night safely and was determined to forget Danny. Maybe this one will be better, Andi told herself. At least she's a woman. She hoped Zemmel would help her sort through all her fears.

"When do I see my shrink?" muttered Andi.

"Oh, he's not going to be in today. He's on an emergency."

"Boy, first he wants me to tell him everything," sputtered Andi, "and then he disappears. I hate this place."

"Why do you hate it so much?"

Andi couldn't bring herself to speak, but her mind raced. How can Dr. Zemmel not be here today, she wanted to scream. I can't keep this in forever.

Aloud, she merely grumbled, "I don't want to talk about it."

Familiar with frustration, Mary tried to soften the blow. "Well, something else is happening."

"What?"

"Your doctor scheduled a visit between you and your parents."

"My parents aren't the ones I want to see."

"Who did you have in mind?"

"My boyfriend, only he isn't really my boyfriend anymore," said Andi, and wondered if Joe would believe her about last night.

Mary started to get the picture. Her new patient seemed a lot like her own fifteen year old daughter. It was hard being a teenager under the best of circumstances and she knew Andi was having a rough time. She sensed the girl's need to talk, but didn't want to provoke her.

"Well, where does your relationship stand right now?" asked Mary cautiously.

"That's the problem. I don't know. When I first got here, I tried to call him and he wouldn't talk to me. But now I hear he's trying to reach me and my doctor won't let me take my calls."

"What about before here?"

Andi was too distracted to answer. She couldn't focus. Mary noticed her dazed expression and changed the subject.

"Ready to go to the bathroom, Andi?"

* * * *

Mary waited outside the lavatory a few minutes, and then grew concerned. The girl was pretty unstable and she wasn't coming out. Mary was reluctant to take away Andi's last bit of privacy, but finally realized it was necessary. When she reached Andi, the girl was staring blankly at nothing, her face covered with tears. Water ran in the sink.

"Andi," called Mary sharply, turn off the water."

Andi watched her fingers manipulate the water faucets. Her hands didn't feel as though they belonged to her. She kept seeing Danny's hands instead of her own. Tell, tell, ached from inside. If you don't tell, you'll go crazy.

"He was so ugly," Andi finally whispered to Mary.

"Who?"

"He put his hands on me," continued Andi, ignoring Mary's question. "Especially my breasts. His big ugly hands were on my breasts. I've got to get out of here. I'm not safe in this hospital."

Mary listened incredulously. "Who?" she asked more insistently, but Andi refused to answer.

Mary thought quickly. The girl was obviously petrified and her anxiety might very well be grounded in reality. There was nothing on her chart that indicated she was prone to fantasizing. But badgering Andi for details at this moment was not appropriate. Mary decided that unconditional affirmation was what Andi needed.

"I believe you, Andi."

"Do you?" sobbed Andi. I didn't think anyone would. This place is awful. I need to get out."

"Where would you rather be right now?" asked Mary calmly.

Andi pictured her room. In it was her desk covered by school books, the white bedspread with tiny pink roses that she wasn't sure that she liked anymore, posters of her favorite rock stars on the walls, her own T.V., V.C.R and C.D. player. But all this offered no comfort.

"I don't want to be anywhere," she confided to Mary. "It doesn't matter where I go. I'll still feel sick."

"I think you're beginning to see there's no getting away from yourself. This place allows you the time and space to deal with the ache you feel inside."

"When the hurt inside gets too big, I can't concentrate on anything else; nothing else matters. Out there nobody thought I should ache. In here, that's all anyone does. I feel it all around. In a way, that scares me cause I can't hide. But I'm glad I don't need to pretend anymore. Are you sure you believe me about what happened last night?"

"Yes Andi, I do.,"

"It was Danny," said Andi quietly. I was sleeping. He woke me up with his hands. At first, I thought it was Joe coming to take me out of here. But as soon as I heard the voice, I knew it was Danny."

"Were you able to see him?"

"Yes, it was Danny's face. He touched me on my breast and then his hands started to move all over me. I got that choking feeling, like I always do when I'm real scared. But this time, I stayed calm. I didn't give in to it. If I did, he wouldn't have stopped. So I made my mind blank. I didn't think of anything but getting rid of him, and then I kicked him in the balls. He doubled over and ran." Even in her grief, there was pride in Andi's voice.

Mary walked her charge back to the cot very slowly, and knew Andi was trying to make peace both inside and outside herself. She also realized that what Andi said about Danny made sense. He was caught stealing drugs and was taken off her case. He could easily have come back to vent his frustrations on a vulnerable patient. I don't care where Zemmel is, she decided, I've got to let him know.

It didn't matter to Andi that her parents were coming. What concerned her most right now was the hospital. Was it good for her, or not? The hospital was different from living at home where she always pushed the truth away, so her mother wouldn't notice. It was a place to talk about things she could never say at home. And that was comforting. But the hospital was also dangerous. She was almost raped! She was scared no one would believe her cause they would think she was crazy.

"Why is life so impossible," Andi finally screamed. "All my parents and Dr. Zemmel want to do is protect me and then I'm almost raped. Of course, I can't yell or tell anyone, 'cause I'm in the nut house. Who'll believe me?"

"You told me."

"Cause I couldn't hold it in. I had to tell. I thought I could hide it, but I was wrong."

"And I believed you. It takes courage to tell the truth. Thanks for trusting me."

Andi lay down on her cot and rolled herself into a ball with her head to her knees. Mary quietly pulled her chair closer to her patient.

"Were you the one who gave me water the night I was in a strait jacket?"

"Yes."

"Don't leave me."

"I won't. You know I'm right here."

Sharon Levine Yedwab

"Will you love me?"
"I'll help you to love yourself."

CHAPTER 13

Bliss stood at the sink and stared at the dirty dishes. Why did she feel so trapped in her own home, she wondered. Marty sat drinking a cup of coffee and reading the paper. This angered her because he didn't appear to share her sense of torment. Finally, she spoke, "You're asking me to betray all my values. I thought I could, but I can't."

"I'm betraying my wife and son," he answered quietly.

"And I suppose I'm your excuse."

"There's no excuse for betrayal."

"So why do you persist?"

Her question unsettled him. He was not used to revealing himself. Committed to a life of probing others, Marty always demanded and managed to receive complete respect for his own privacy. Bliss challenged him to share where he never considered the possibility with anyone other than a professional. But he welcomed her persistence.

"Because I desire intimacy," he whispered.

She finally turned from the sink and looked at him directly. His words voiced her own turmoil. Bliss also craved the warmth of a close relationship even if it challenged her value system.

"I know you're a very private man," Bliss said more gently, "but I want to share your solitude."

"We will share," he promised and kissed her.

Together, they entered her bedroom and undressed very slowly in the late morning sunlight. Bliss relished his nakedness and caressed him with her lips, and he hardened beneath her touch. The warmth of her body overwhelmed Marty's rational thinking. He immersed himself in pleasurable feelings that he didn't wish to question. There was a mystery to every aspect of her body and he wanted to slowly comprehend it and make it his. Their legs were intertwined and the curve of her muscles excited him. Even the touch of her ankle on his stimulated desire.

"You're very beautiful," he whispered, and kissed her breasts.

"You're touching the softest part of me," she sighed, "and I'm powerless to stop you."

He was inspired by her. He longed to capture her complexity. "My power stems from yours," he answered with new virility, and slowly twisted her body so she knelt beneath him and they no longer faced each other. He nuzzled the small of her back and moved relentlessly between her thighs.

"I am nothing; you are everything," Bliss groaned.

"Why do you call yourself nothing," he asked and squeezed her nipple, "when you are so beautiful?"

Her vagina tightened around him. Excitement stirred through Marty. He ran his fingers along her leg and Bliss shivered at his touch. His pounding rhythm increased. His knees spread her thighs apart.

She enjoyed the vitality of his nature—the strength of his passion.

"I want to come! Now! Right now!" she commanded.

Her words fired his desire; he tightened and engulfed her in a blinding moment of oneness.

And then she flung him off! Her legs cramped. She needed space. His body too was suddenly oppressed by hers. But they were not offended by each other. He reached for her and lightly kissed her hair. Intensity still lingered.

*　　*　　*　　*

Anne Zemmel sat with her feet swiveled into an upward position, conducive to alleviating the lower back pain she sometimes endured. The room in the rear of her home, where she managed various volunteer projects, was professionally redecorated every two years. But this year, she was exceptionally pleased with the muted color coordination of the room because she actively chose the colors herself, rather than put complete reliance on an interior decorator. Too bad Marty refuses to allow me to help him with his den, she mused. It's always so dark and murky.

Anne rarely entered Marty's sanctuary, as he called it, but was never quite sure if that was her choice or his. Thoughts of Marty quickly ran beyond color scheme, and unhappiness pricked her. Marty never came home last night. There was nothing new in that, but there was a subtle change in his attitude.

Marty often ran late at the hospital, and even slept there, but they rarely discussed it. He expected her to understand and she did. Eventually, she trained herself to be indifferent. It was no secret to either of them that they were caught up in separate lives after 27 years of a mostly cool marriage. But lately, he punctuated his absences with unusual fervency. He was obviously intent on obtaining her acceptance of his alibis. Why all this unusual concern, she wondered cynically. My feelings aren't suddenly important to him after all these years. He's developed a new passion, she wisely surmised. Something he needs me to forgive.

This last thought exhausted Anne. What hurt even more than her husband's possible infidelity was the awareness that she could not share her fears with anyone. What she realized now was that her relationships with other women were little more than superficial. She was certainly respected, but was she liked? This new look at herself cut into the prestige she often substituted for friendship, and made her lonely.

Anne was trapped in a twilight of half knowledge and this lent itself to a state of vulnerability. Sleeping fears began to awaken as her self-examination progressed. The security of her material possessions could no longer protect her from a repressed level of awareness. In fact, the muted colors of the room worked to create a mood of relaxation that enabled her to concentrate on disturbing thoughts despite her anxiety.

Marty was always the knowing psychiatrist. Even before he received his degrees, he seemed to know everything. Anne secretly harbored a sense of inferiority because she graduated from a state school with a B.A. in Education. The fact that she couldn't understand life as he did was a basic tenet of their relationship. She often fantasized that she was not able to see him with the same clarity with which he envisioned her. And then there was that private side to him, the part she never dared enter.

Once, when they were newlyweds, she opened a piece of his mail. It wasn't anything from the hospital according to the return address, so she assumed it would be all right. He often called and instructed her to open certain types of mail similar to that one. Marty came home late that night and immediately asked for his correspondence. When he spotted the opened envelope, he snapped, "How dare you?" and smacked her in the face. She was too stunned to cry or even question him. Who will believe me, she asked herself. They'll say he's a doctor. They'll say he's dedicated to healing; not hurting. There was no one to turn to that night either, she recalled. But he never hit me again, she mused further. He was careful to rule his passion with an iron fist after that. Maybe that's where his coldness came from. When they were younger, she always thought of Marty as different, but never distant. She liked the fact that he was different.

They both grew up in that horrible neighborhood she couldn't wait to leave, but she didn't meet Marty until after high school. She was surprised that although Marty held a large scholarship to an out-of-town prestigious school, he made it a point to come home on as many weekends as possible. Somehow, he loved the neighborhood and he loved her. And that was fine because, within days of their meeting, she was madly in love with him. They shared a passion to change the world and they were sure they made an unbeatable combination. But we never really changed anything, Anne sighed to herself. Only we changed. Her fingers automatically traveled to the wrinkled skin around her eyes, where she found what for her was the inevitable stamp of age and ugliness—crow's feet. There they were, and there they would remain, a constant reminder that she was no longer young. After all, I've got a 28 year old son, Anne reminded herself, and then her thoughts turned to Allen. The year Allen turned 12 was when her marriage permanently soured. However, Marty's conflicts with Allen began when the boy reached 10 and started thinking on his own. Anne always maintained that their problems started with boxing. Marty could never accept Allen's dislike of the sport. Whenever Marty managed to convince Allen to accompany him to the gym for sparring practice, the boy was squeamish. He said the place was decrepit and he hated the smell.

Allen's aloofness hurt Marty deeply because he was sure it was really for him. Just as the neighborhood kids rejected him years ago, now his own son was repulsed. However, these fears were too painful for Marty to contemplate, so he hid them from himself, but he couldn't hide them from Anne.

This unresolved conflict eventually escalated, and by the time Allen was 12, he and Marty fought about everything. And Anne was always in the middle. She tried to discuss Allen with Marty, but he insisted that Allen was purely recalcitrant. He staunchly refused to listen to any of her ideas on the subject. Marty even went so far as to mock Anne for being a nag if she pressed him too far.

Anne grew increasingly infuriated with Marty's behavior and eventually sought outside help. When she and Allen began regular therapy, Marty regarded it as a betrayal of his expertise and would not go to the sessions.

Therapy never stopped the fighting between Marty and Allen, so they began moving away from each other. Anne gave up trying to bring them together, and did her best to maintain separate relationships. It was easier that way.

These unhappy thoughts caused Anne to pour herself a scotch despite the early morning hour, but the drink calmed her nerves and soon she stopped dwelling on Allen and Marty. She didn't like to think of herself as drinking like this, but the taste was smooth and the mellow feeling was comforting.

It was in the midst of these relaxed feelings that Anne remembered her sprained ankle. The ankle was almost fully healed and forgotten, but suddenly there was meaning attached to it. There's something about that ankle that connects to Marty, nagged a thought somewhere in the back of her consciousness. But what, she wondered, and realized that she was seriously afraid to answer that question.

"Ma'am, Ma'am er...uh," came an intruding voice.

"Oh, Lilly, I'm sorry. I didn't hear you come in."

"I knocked several times, but you didn't answer," continued the maid in a voice that Anne thought might be a condemnation of her early morning drink.

Anne wasn't sure if Lilly noticed her fairly recent daytime drinking habit and immediately wondered if perhaps she wanted the maid to scold her. There was an embarrassing pause between the two women who seemed for that moment more equal than usual.

"I, uh, guess I was just lost in thought," Anne finally offered.

"I get that way myself," answered Lilly, making sure her facial expression revealed nothing of what she was thinking. "I'm getting the house ready for the window cleaner. He should be here any minute."

Although Lilly worked for the Zemmels for the past 10 years and sometimes seemed more at home in their home than they did, she purposely did not let Anne know that she was on to her drinking. She enjoyed a sense of pride and security in her work and chose not to endanger her position by becoming too personal. Lilly didn't want her relationship with Anne to be shattered by an instability that she clearly deemed to be none of her business.

Windows and cleaning were far from Anne, who envied Lilly for the first time since she'd hired her. Lilly was able to see the fine old home in all its physical stature and grace, while Anne was left to tend the emptiness.

Lilly began to putter about the room and Anne quickly forgot she was there. What about the ankle, Anne nagged at herself once more. That's when I began to notice a change in Marty, she thought darkly. Lilly quietly shut the door behind her, but Anne was oblivious, as she almost hypnotically began to reconstruct events.

Anne remembered a Bike-A-Thon for Soviet Jewry in the City. She was supposed to go on a Sunday afternoon. But the night before the event, she twisted her ankle and begged Marty to take her place. He came home from the event later than she expected he would, but Marty was never on time. Ironically, her suspicions were only aroused by a steady stream of excuses that began to flow after that Sunday.

Anne's fingers involuntarily went to the wrinkles around her eyes, and this time they were wet. Marty was physically hers. All these years, he belonged to her. She could not even imagine life without him.

Am I hearing things, she wondered through jangled nerves. Why is there screaming in the hallway? She opened her mouth to call Lilly, but closed it almost immediately when she recognized the window cleaner's voice.

"You got too many windows, lady."

"And you call yourself a window cleaner," came Lilly's fiercely sarcastic reply.

Suddenly, Anne was uncertain of who controlled the house.

And make sure you shine 'em up real good," continued Lilly. "These front windows are a showpiece." The quiet perfection of Anne's room was marred. Even the comfort of alcohol refused to soothe her dejection. "How much longer will this even be my room," she brooded.

CHAPTER 14

"I told you, I ain't goin' to no school," Yolanda shouted at Rose.

Sandy Glover heard the noise outside her classroom and walked over to the girl, "What's going on here? Why are you screaming?"

"Look, I don't belong here Miss. I'm not stayin' on no funny farm."

Gently, Ms. Glover asked her name.

"My name's Bubba, Miss."

"No, I mean what's your real name; not some junk street name."

Yolanda was startled by the teacher's manner and simply stated her full name.

"Well, come into the classroom, Yolanda and we'll try to piece this thing together."

Rose Schneider was relieved. "Thanks Sandi," she said. "Here's her chart."

Yolanda was calmed by the teacher's demeanor and followed her into the classroom.

"O.K. Yolanda," Ms. Glover came straight to the point, "why don't you think you belong here?"

"Cause they wanted to put me into Irvington General, but it was full. That's the only reason I ended up in this place."

"That's all quite true," commented Ms Glover, "but according to your chart, you were going into the psychiatric unit of Irvington General. That's the same as here."

Yolanda's face fell when she heard these words. "Why'd they wanna do that to me? I was only fighting."

"You've been fighting an awful lot from what I see here, and you need support. So, why don't you take a seat and join the class."

The class was in the middle of a geography lesson and Ms. Glover handed Yolanda a map with some magic markers.

"Oh, I like maps Miss," announced Yolanda with a surprisingly pleasant smile."

"Great, now we're getting somewhere."

Just then, Andi entered with Mary. Ms. Glover was surprised when she didn't see Danny, but she simply motioned Andi to a seat.

"We're having a geography lesson Andi," said Mr. Glover, casually trying to ease the tension she sensed in her student.

"Ugh," thought Andi, who hated maps passionately ever since her notorious U.S. History I class. "I feel kinda tired," she muttered.

"Come on Andi, let's give it a try," coaxed Ms. Glover, handing her a map and magic markers. "Start filling in countries and capitals of Eastern Europe. There's a code to follow on the side."

"Pst," whispered Tina as Ms. Glover walked away, "Why're ya so late?"

"I kinda spaced out in the bathroom," replied Andi.

"Still thinkin' 'bout that guy?"

"Huh?" answered Andi in a daze. "Oh, you mean Joe."

"Yeah, who else?"

Andi didn't want to answer, so she turned to Ms. Glover and was immediately struck by the flamboyance of her outfit. Sandi Glover purposely used a lot of color to drown out the institutional drab and today she was wearing a silver blouse with a magenta full length skirt. Dangling turquoise earrings completed her attire and, although it wasn't exactly Andi's style, she decided she liked it. Ms. Glover noticed Andi's attention, but decided to ignore it and instead focused on Carlos. "That's a great job," she commented looking over his shoulder.

"What about me?" chimed in Yolanda very unexpectedly.

"Oh Bubba, you've hardly done anything," jibed Tina.

"Tina," said Ms. Glover sharply, "we're calling our new student by her real name, Yolanda. Let's have pride in our names and in ourselves. Furthermore, Tina, you needn't be such a busybody." Turning to Yolanda, Ms. Glover continued, "You're doing a great job, Yolanda, but keep working. You've got a long way to go."

Andi was reminded of her real classrooms with rows of desks, green blackboards and American flags. But the faces all looked blank. Would her friends miss her? She couldn't visualize them. Would they call her retarded?

"Where are you right now?" asked Ms. Glover when she saw Andi drifting.

"Nowhere. I guess I was thinking about my real school."

"Would you like to draw a picture of it?"

"Uh, maybe." She pictured the auditorium; the blackness of the empty stage, the quiet empty seats.

"Use your imagination," encouraged the teacher as she put paper in front of Andi and a magic marker in her hand.

The stage was so big, the kids looked small. School was out for vacation, but the cast of the school play met for rehearsals. So quiet, so exciting. Especially after the wedding scene, when Michael kissed her again and again. She started to see his face and began drawing. Andi wanted to draw Michael kissing her. It felt good. But she knew she wasn't drawing him. Rather, she was drawing someone she didn't want to think about.

I need red, lots of red, Andi thought, picking out the red marker. For the blood. I'm really gonna make him bleed.

"My G-d Andi, what are you drawing?" whispered Tina. "It looks like, Danny! And he's all cut up, Andi, why isn't he here today?" Andi didn't answer.

"Andi, talk to me," persisted Tina.

"His hand," was all Andi could say.

"What about his hand?"

Andi said nothing more and continued drawing. Will Tina believe me, she wondered.

"Ms Glover, is it journal writing time yet?" asked Tina while she eyed Andi stabbing at her paper with the red marker.

"Whenever you're ready."

"Journals?" questioned Yolanda, "I ain't hardly finished my map. Who needs journals?"

"Journals are to record your thoughts."

"Journals are stupid," said a voice that Andi hadn't heard before.

"In journals, you can write down things you'd never dare say to anyone else," interjected Carlos.

"I say anything I want to say," retorted Yolanda. "If I don't like you, I let you know to your face. I don't need to put it into no journal. In fact, I hate writin' more than anything."

"Well, let's look at this as a new experience for you, Yolanda," said Ms. Glover diplomatically.

"But I don't know what to say."

"Why don't you start by writing about your name. Write about why you prefer a nickname."

Andi joined in almost against her will, "I don't like my name either."

"O.K., Andi, that's something for you to write about also."

"Hey," said Yolanda like a cat who just caught a bird, "why don't you make Andi use her full name?"

For a moment the class was very still. Fairness was paramount with Ms. Glover, who always stressed equality. The girl was right. Both of them were using nicknames. Why did she consider one better than the other?

"You got me there, Yolanda. I guess I didn't think Bubba gave you a very good feeling about yourself. It has nothing to do with your real name."

"What's so good about Andi?" asked Yolanda.

"It's a variation of Andrea," answered Jerry. Everyone stared at him. He almost never spoke.

"In here, I'll be Yolanda, "the girl finally decided," but outside I'm still Bubba."

Her words lifted the tension and everyone began writing. Andi knew she was writing the same thing over and over, but she didn't dare read it. Rather, she surreptitiously handed her paper to Tina who read it and paled. "Danny almost raped me," was scrawled all over the sheet.

The girls stared at each other.

"How did you stop him?" Tina finally asked.

"I kicked him in the balls and he ran."

"Radical," was all Tina could think of, but Andi caught her admiration and enjoyed it. True, she was attacked, but she was able to take care of herself. And almost as important, people believed her. Maybe my life's shit, she thought, but it's mine. No one's gonna take it away. Not even me!

Seated next to Andi, Yolanda was deep in thought. She rarely attended school on a daily basis and wasn't eager to relate to paper and pen. But she liked the teacher and that made a difference in her motivation. Ms. Glover was strict, but Yolanda believed she cared and that was important. Ms. Glover made her feel like she counted. Why do most people think I'm a blob, mused Yolanda. I bet they call me Bubba because I'm so fat. She recalled that awful scale in the nurse's office. She hated when everyone lined up to be weighed. As soon as she stepped on the scale, there were always snickers.

CHAPTER 15

Bliss woke up first and disentangled herself from Marty. She was entranced with him, and was sure he was everything she ever desired in a man. Yet within all that tantalizing perfection lived an even greater imperfection. She ached with censure as she thought of his marriage. Although she wanted to encircle his still sleeping body in her hungry arms, every fiber told her she was wrong. The cruelty of temptation stabbed her heart and she began to chastise herself.

I'm destroying myself with him, she told the ceiling mirror that was suddenly staring down at her.

Are you really? I thought you were tired of conventional relationships, answered her reflection.

I am, she admitted to herself. I'm always on the outside of things. There's never any intimacy.

But are you willing to risk the hurt, the mirror asked perceptively. What about the pain that will ultimately befall you?

That's the problem. I'm scared, Bliss mused and felt like an initiate on a quest of forbidden knowledge.

Imagination squelched fear until she rose from the bed and glanced at Marty again. He was sleeping, while she couldn't. Who was he anyway? How could she let him sleep in her bed? Suddenly, she didn't want to be there. Bliss dressed quickly and took flight into the anonymity of the city.

*   *   *   *

Marty was awakened by his beeper. Where's Bliss, he half wondered as he called the hospital.

"Danny attacked Andi and another nurse," a voice on the other end said. "Andi's shaken up, but she managed to scare him off."

"I should have seen it coming," he muttered. "I'll be in immediately."

As he dressed, Marty poured himself a glass of juice and hoped his suit wasn't too wrinkled. Where's the hell's Bliss?

Marty was so rushed, he forgot his fear of elevators and stepped inside the iron tomb. To his astonishment, it actually worked. He thought of Bliss again, but only for an instant. I should have handled Danny much differently. I just never figured that schmuck to go beyond drugs——to go on the attack. Where did Andi find the strength to fight him off, he thought admiringly. That kid's really got guts.

* * * *

Andi walked into the visitor's area to greet her parents. She was glad Mary was with her. It wasn't going to be easy and she wanted all the support she could muster. Andi was fairly certain that whatever strength she gained in the hospital would be ultimately zapped by the end of the visit, but she also knew she couldn't hide forever.

One thing was certain. She wasn't prepared to die, and in therapy she chose life. Her choice now lay in the way she would live. Either she would control herself and her actions or others would do it for her. Dr. Zemmel said once control was established, there were more choices concerning happiness, and what was really important to her. How could she share these ideas with those she loved? Would she ever make her family understand a process that was completely foreign to them?

Andi predicted inevitable frustration and feared meeting her parents. She was too naked to be with them, and was sure the visit would end in a screaming match. I'm nauseous. What if I throw up all over the floor, she asked herself.

When Andi finally spotted her parents in a far corner, talking with Dr. Zemmel, she wanted to run in the other direction. But she fought her nausea and simply asked Mary, "What's Dr. Zemmel doing here? I thought he was on an emergency."

"I called him about what happened to you."

"And he believed me?"

"Yes."

"What do you think my parents will say?"

"I guess you'll find out. Go and meet them. I'll wait here."

One foot followed the other and Andi stood before her parents, "Hi Mom! Hi Dad!"

Andi's parents thought they were fairly prepared for the visit until they spoke with Dr. Zemmel. Ed and Sarah were completely unnerved by Andi's encounter with the male nurse Zemmel put in charge of her. How could they leave her here?

When Ed looked up at his daughter, he wondered at her composure. Why wasn't she hysterical?

Sarah noticed Andi's weight loss, but was too shattered to speak. Andi must really hate me for this was all she could think.

"So Andi," began Ed carefully, "It's been awhile."

"It's only been a few days," countered Andi, "but I guess a lot's happened."

"We just heard from Dr. Zemmel," answered Levy.

"Andi," blurted Sarah, "you can't stay. I want Dr. Zemmel to discharge you immediately."

"Mrs. Levy," interjected Zemmel, "I thought we agreed..."

"I didn't agree to anything," snapped Sarah. "Look at her. Look at this place. What kind of parents are we anyway?"

"Can't you think of anyone but you?" asked Andi. "First you threw me in here. Now you want to yank me out. Doesn't anyone care about what I have to say?"

Ed looked at his daughter with new respect.

"I want to hear what you have to say, Andi. But we also want to know that you're alright. When your mother and I heard that you were almost...almost..."

"Raped," said Andi.

"We didn't think you'd want to remain here and frankly we don't think you should."

"It's like there's no place for me anywhere," whispered Andi. "I'm not ready to go home. There's too much blood there."

"Andi," said Dr. Zemmel gently, "you weren't the only one Danny attacked last night. He's been positively identified by a nurse and is under arrest. Security in the hospital is increased. I've assured your parents that you will be safe here. I told them that I don't think you should leave."

"I don't want to," she answered quietly.

Sarah and Ed looked uncomfortably at each other.

"Can we see our daughter alone?" Sarah asked.

"Of course," answered Zemmel and left.

"I'm not a baby," said Andi when Zemmel was out of earshot. "Don't treat me like one."

"But it may not be safe here," insisted Sarah.

"They put on extra security, Sar," interjected Ed half-heartedly.

"He was her nurse!"

"Mom, Dad, you're missing the point. I took care of myself. That's what's important to me. Yes, I was terrified, but I didn't go under. I pulled myself together and I fought back. Doesn't that mean anything to you?" Her parents just stared at her.

"Can we talk about something else?" Andi finally asked.

"Such as?"

"Such as they won't let me make phone calls."

"We know," answered Ed quietly.

"But Dr. Zemmel won't let me receive calls either."

"Who's been calling?" asked Sarah.

"Joe."

"How do you know."

"My friend told me."

"A girl in here?"

"Yeah!"

Finding themselves in dangerous territory with no convenient escape hatch, Andi's parents gaped at her and were afraid to speak. Andi interpreted silence as possible acceptance, and continued to plead her cause, "At first, I thought it was your fault. I imagined you were trying to break it up between Joe and me."

"Isn't it kind of over between the two of you?" interjected Ed as gently as possible.

"True, we were cooling it, Dad. But to me it was never completely over. So when I heard Joe dated someone else, I really overreacted."

Sarah guiltily remembered how relieved she was about that cooling off period. Her daughter's heart was broken and she ignored it; only aware of her own values. "However, this is completely out of our hands," said Sarah, thinking out loud. "Dr. Zemmel stopped Joe's calls on his own, assuming what your friend said is true."

"Yeah, but I bet you're glad," grimaced Andi in anger. Ed glanced in Mary's direction for help and was amazed to see her dozing. With the realization they were on their own, he desperately tried to steer his family into shallow water, "So, how's school here Andi? Are you keeping up with your studies?"

"Stop trying to change the subject. Don't you care about what this doctor is doing to me?"

"Andi," cried Sarah, desperately, "You just said you wanted to stay here. Dad was wrong to cut you off like that, but he just doesn't want you to be upset. We love you and want you to get well."

"If you love me, start seeing things from my point of view. Start respecting my values."

Ed tried to reason with his daughter, "Andi, we're willing to listen. That's why we're here. But please keep it down."

"I'm not going to keep it down," cried Andi in a steadily rising voice. "This family's a G-d damn joke. Boy, Mom, you're happy it's out of your hands. How convenient for you. Don't hide behind that psychiatrist. Sure, he makes rules; that's his job. But you're my parents. You claim you love me. If you really do, you'll make him change his mind."

"Andi," pleaded Sarah, "what do you want us to do? Stop yelling and talk to us."

"Let me return Joe's call."

"But he hurt you so much, Andi. We can't possibly ignore what happened," argued Sarah.

"Don't try to fool me. Your only concern is that he`s not Jewish."

Sarah said nothing, and resigned herself to her daughter's vehemence.

"Andi," said Ed evenly, "it's unfair for you to say our actions stem totally from religion. We never prevented you from dating him, although we didn't approve. As a matter of fact, he spent several evenings in our home, and to my recollection your mother and I were quite hospitable. There is no question that we did not give you the support you needed when things got tough, but your mother and I are no longer blind to your suffering. We want to help you go beyond it. Unfortunately, Joe didn't treat you very well and your devastation concerns us very much. Dr. Zemmel doesn't want you to talk to Joe because he doesn't want you getting upset. His decision has absolutely nothing to do with religion."

"But look at me," shrieked Andi, "I'm worse than upset. I have nothing to live for."

"You do darling, you do," cried Sarah.

"Without Joe, there's nothing left for me," sobbed Andi.

Sarah began to shake her daughter's thin shoulders while Ed ran toward Mary.

Mary woke up with a start and saw Levy approaching her. What happened? Oh G-d, I fell asleep; she remembered her drinking binge from the night before.

"My wife and daughter...." began Levy.

"They look like they're hugging each other," said Mary and wondered if her vision was impaired.

"Are you sure? My daughter is very upset about her ex-boyfriend."

"That may be true, but I think your wife and daughter are bonding."

Mary and Ed walked slowly to Andi. "Visiting hours are over," announced Mary quietly.

Andi refused to let go of her mother. She wasn't about to forgive her, but the warmth felt good. She needed it desperately.

"Dad, will you talk to Dr. Zemmel about Joe's call?" she pleaded, still holding onto Sarah's arms.

"I'm going to talk to Zemmel," he assured Andi.

"Promise."

"I promise, I promise." answered Ed with exasperation.

Slowly, mother and daughter disengaged from their embrace.

"Mom..."

"Yes?"

"I was really frightened last night. After he ran off, I couldn't yell. I was scared no one would believe me. All I could see were his hands...his dirty, filthy, rotten hands all over me."

"Andi, honey," began Ed.

"Let her talk Mr. Levy," interrupted Mary. "It's important for her to talk about it."

"I lay in hell after he left. I was so scared he'd come back."

"We have to have faith that he's not coming back," said Sarah.

"He was my nurse Ma," sobbed Andi. "I trusted him."

Mary supported Andi and motioned her parents to leave. There were no more words Sarah could think of to comfort her daughter. It seemed impossible to leave Andi like this; to go home without her.

CHAPTER 16

Though Bliss traveled a great deal on subways, she was still fascinated by them. It was kind of a love-hate relationship. She liked the speed going in and out of darkness, but she feared the third rail. She dreaded the thought of a mechanical breakdown, yet found the pulsating noise exciting. She was afraid that her fellow passengers might mug or rape her, but she still liked to watch them.

She noticed the guy seated diagonally across from her was physically attractive. He was very blond and muscular with high cheekbones. His eyes squinted and there was a macho ruggedness to his features. Bliss couldn't help looking up from the magazine she wasn't reading to glance at him sideways. The mole on his left cheek reminded her of her ex-husband. He even looked like Craig around the eyes.

She hated herself for running to Craig when things got rough, but she couldn't break the pattern. She knew where he ate lunch and that's where she was going. He listened a lot more objectively since their divorce.

Divorced two years, Bliss still was far from independent. She conducted a fairly prestigious career as an accountant on the outside, but inside there was only instability. Her ex-marriage paradoxically was now a safe port; like home to a college kid when there's no place else to go.

Bliss glanced at the advertisements above the window directly across from her seat. She enjoyed figuring out the Spanish. Just recently, she learned that SIDA meant AIDS. But today a homeless child from Nicaragua captured her attention. Perhaps because it was juxtaposed against a huge Nathan's hot dog.

Bliss's thoughts eventually sprinted to Marty. There was an icy aloofness about him that both intrigued and scared her. Her ex-husband, was easily manipulated through his anger, but Marty never lost himself in rage. He always found a way to smooth around the edges through conversation, which usually resulted in her heightened vulnerability. That was it! She was very fragile with him, which would probably be welcome if he wasn't married. But he was. There was no getting around it and she could never withstand such an emotionally devastating relationship. So, like a homing pigeon, she headed for Craig and despised him for allowing it. The red danger signals on the subway tunnel looked like they blinked for her.

The reverie broke when Bliss noticed the hulk across the aisle masturbating. Is this his way of approaching me, she wondered in disgust. Is that all men want? Is that what Marty really wants? Off the subway, Bliss mindlessly rode the escalator to the Port Authority. Men and women were strewn everywhere like human litter. Is there any difference between us? Where's my new wonderful life?

She took the escalator and headed mechanically for steps leading to the Newark bus. The fumes hit her nostrils with a sense of utter futility. I'm scared to death, she slowly admitted to herself. Every time I get the tiniest glimpse of new life, I run back to Jersey. Marty can be the biggest shit in the world, but why am I running away? It's my damn apartment! Why am I sneaking out like some high school kid? I'm making Craig into a parent who's gonna pat me on the head and tell me everything's O.K. Well, if he couldn't give me support the first time around, how can I fall for this stupid sham?

She watched the bus fill up and forced herself to stand aside, while her inner voice clamored. Caught in the stillness of a dream state, she watched the movement of others. Their action took the place of hers. Her eyes moved rapidly from scene to scene and Bliss envied a sense of purpose in the other passengers. She jealously clung to their every move. There was a man jabbering in a foreign language, trying to get three huge suitcases on luggage racks, while his wife supervised the children who hunted for the best seats nearest the windows.

Following them were two elderly women in Sunday straw flowered hats, helping each other up the three high steps of the bus.

Devoid of their purpose, Bliss realized she shared little with them. They were all going; she was just running away. She decided to return home. Slowly, her feet retraced the steps away from the heaviest fumes, down the escalator and back into the subway.

Bliss clutched the strap in the subway car and once again enjoyed moving in and out of darkness at top speeds. Her thoughts drifted to danger. She craved it like some who devoured salt as a life support. With Marty there were zillions of risks. There was also the challenge of his personality. Endlessly intrigued by his need for privacy to the exclusion of all else, she was even willing to loosen her morals. Well, maybe morality is a standard to strive for and never actually achieve, she told herself, as she stepped from the dankness of the subway tunnel and walked home.

Was it her imagination, or was that Marty sitting on the steps of her building? "Hi," he grinned sheepishly, rising to greet her. "The truth is, I just wanted to see you again."

Acknowledging his fear of elevators, she climbed the back steps with him. Out of breath by the third landing, they paused.

"Why are you so afraid of elevators?" she laughed teasingly. "You're a shrink. Aren't you in the business of curing phobias rather than giving in to them?"

"Why are you so afraid of me?" he countered.

"Why must you always answer questions with questions?" she asked, searching for her key.

"Why don't you answer them?" he called down to her as he reached the apartment first.

"Here's the key...catch," she called back.

Opening her door, he was again struck by the confusion. "Yeah, it's kind of a wreck," she admitted reading his thoughts. "I wish I could blame it on my son, but most of this is mine."

She moved to the stove quickly and offered him coffee. When he refused, she skipped formalities and got to the point, "What are you doing here anyway?"

"Why did you leave?"

"I asked first."

Deadlocked, they knew there were no easy answers to either of their questions.

"O.K.," he said, unable to avoid taking the initiative, "obviously I have no right to be here. I just want to be."

"This is beginning to hurt a great deal. I'm very attracted to you, but I'm frightened. What about your wife? Doesn't she think you're strange lately?"

"She's very busy with her own life."

"What about last night. You never went home."

"She had an all-night bender of `Save the World from Something or Other'."

Bliss was surprised at the sarcasm. "I thought you were also interested in helping people."

"I am, but now I'm more interested in saving myself right here with you."

That really sounded like a line and Bliss was actually grateful for the sound of her buzzer.

"Excuse me," she said, going to a box in the alcove. "Yes, who is it?"

"Chaim Katz from the `Yeshiva Mitzvah Campaign,' a campaign of good deeds. We're going to all our Jewish neighbors and asking for charity. We have literature as well. May I come up?"

"How do you know who's Jewish?"

"That's easy; we just read the names on the mailboxes."

Bliss invited him to come upstairs, glad for the interruption.

CHAPTER 17

Andi was almost lighthearted at supper. The catharsis with her mother was a relief, and her father seemed more understanding. She was so sure he would help that she confided in her friends.

"Guess what? My Dad's gonna talk to my shrink about letting me call Joe."

Shooting a cynical glance at her, Tina was skeptical.

"Did he actually say that?"

"Not exactly."

"So, how can you be so sure."

"Look Tina, he's my father. I know him."

"Do you?" asked Tina curtly. "I never really knew mine."

"Me neither," said Yolanda.

"Well, I guess I knew my father when I was really little," continued Tina. "But I've rarely seen him since I was three. He doesn't live in the area. And when I do see him, it's worse than nothing. All he ever asks me about is my report card."

"My father lives right down the street from us, but he might as well be in another country. He doesn't want to be bothered with me or my mother," said Yolanda.

"Do you have a stepfather, Bubba?" asked Andi.

"No, thank G-d! My mom's bringing us kids up by herself."

"Well I do," said Tina heatedly, "and it's a mutual hate society."

"This is gettin' too morbid," said Yolanda. "How'd we get on this topic anyway?"

"I was talking about my father and how I trusted him...", said Andi.

"Well, that's your problem," said Yolanda flatly.

"We were talking about Andi and her boyfriend," said Tina, her face brightening, "and I have an idea to get them together."

Immediately, Andi panicked. She only wanted to call Joe. She wasn't sure if she actually wanted to see him.

"Quiet," whispered Yolanda, jerking her head in Mary's direction, "her nurse will hear you."

"It's O.K.," said Tina, "they're changing shifts."

"Just like a jail," sighed Yolanda.

"Just give me his phone number, Andi. I have access to everything," said Tina.

Andi hesitated, jarred at the thought of Joe talking to anyone but her. What did Tina really want with Joe? "What would you say to him?" she asked.

"I'd invite him here."

"Here?" exclaimed Andi. "I'm a prisoner. I can't even make phone calls. A nurse watches me 24 hours a day."

"Then you'll meet him in the park next door," answered Tina blithely.

Things were moving along too quickly for Andi, and in the back of her mind there was more doubt than certainty. Can I really handle seeing Joe, she wondered again. Is the park safe? Will Danny be hiding there?

But it felt good to be part of the conspiracy, so she courageously rode the wave, "Let's do it!"

"When shall we plan for?" asked Tina.

"Is today Monday?" wondered Andi, aware that she wasn't keeping very good track of time.

"No, Tuesday," said Yolanda.

"One day sure seems like the next in here." complained Andi... well why not make it next Sunday."

"Good idea," agreed Tina warmly. "Sundays are slower, with less staff."

"O.K., so you have the day," said Yolanda, playing devil's advocate, "but what about the place? How you gonna sneak Andi out of here?"

"We can steal some props," suggested Tina. "Like uniforms and a stretcher or something."

"I'm beginning to see why you're in a nut house," laughed Yolanda. But she had to admit, it sounded like an adventure.

"I know," continued Tina, "we'll wrap Andi up in a garbage bag and say she's goin' down for electric shock therapy."

"Do they really have that here?" asked Yolanda.

"Sure. Want some?" asked Tina and grabbed her arm, "Buzz!"

By now even Andi was laughing. "Tina, you're really nuts! They're gonna haul you off for some extra treatments right now. But really, I'm under lock and key. How are you two gonna get me outta here?"

"She can't even pee alone," added Yolanda.

"What do you guys have to lose?" insisted Tina. "The worst thing is we fail and that's no big deal around here."

"What about the electric shock?" asked Yolanda darkly.

"Oh, get a life; don't be nerds. Where's the fun without the risk?"

Tina couldn't quite explain it, but Andi's struggle was becoming hers. Confronting Andi's fear was a way of encountering her own. Tina needed release after three months of restricted living, yet she was just as afraid of leaving the institution as she was of remaining in it. In fact, as she planned Andi's departure, Tina was afraid to take a weekend pass home.

Andi glanced up and spotted her night watch approaching. "Shhh," she whispered, savoring the danger of the moment.

"Hi girls, how's it going?"

"Hello," they mumbled, their heartbeats quickened by intrigue. Under the table Tina gently tapped Yolanda who tapped Andi.

"Our pact is sealed," she whispered.

Like blood brothers, thought Andi, and enjoyed the togetherness. She just wasn't sure about Joe...or herself...or anything.

CHAPTER 18

Ed Levy was fifteen minutes early for his 10 o'clock appointment with Dr. Zemmel. At least he has an office outside the hospital, he noted. Like you should be grateful, he retorted to himself. Where's your control? When did life suddenly become a string of doctor's visits? Since my wife's a religious fanatic and my daughter attempted suicide.

Ed recalled how Andi was his baby before her Bat Mitzvah. Life really changed after that. Things were no longer simple. There was a new anger in her. It tinged every aspect of family life. Suddenly Andi hated everything—even her name!

Ed knew about anger and frustration. He and Sarah often ran into communication problems. He accused her of being narrow minded and she said he never listened. Before Sarah, he had conflicts with his parents who disagreed with his anti-Viet Nam politics.

Sometimes Ed would see himself in Andi. She can work it out, he'd tell himself. All she needs is space. But then he'd admit that Sarah would never give her that kind of space. If he intervened too strongly on Andi's behalf, it would mean a fight with his wife, and he didn't want one. So he hid behind his newspapers and tried not to listen. But in Zemmel's waiting room, their voices haunted him:

"Andi, Joe's not Jewish," Sarah usually began.

"If I can choose my girlfriends regardless of religion, why can't I date whoever I like?" Andi challenged her mother.

"Because you have to think of your future," was Sarah's cryptic reply, which infuriated her daughter.

"What does going to the movies have to do with my future? I don't even know if I want to get married. Don't you believe in fun?"

Levy almost jumped when he heard Zemmel call his name. "Oh," he apologized, extending his arm, "I was just kicking a few thoughts around."

"Good morning," smiled Zemmel and ushered Levy into his office.

"This is hard for me. I've never talked with a..."

"Shrink before?"

"Yeah. Look...my daughter seems to like you and that's important to us, but we're still not sure about the hospital."

"I understand your concern, but we're handling security. Is that the only reason you're here?"

"Well, there is something else I want to discuss. Uh...I feel really awkward. I'm not sure how to start."

He looked to Marty for help but only got a stare. So, he clenched his fists and continued, "I don't think my daughter's a virgin...my wife doesn't know," he added quickly, paused and started to speak once more. "Andi really fell for this Joe in a big way. They were in several classes together plus lunch."

"Why do you feel your daughter's not a virgin?" asked Zemmel curiously.

Ed was flustered by the question and answered slowly, "Actually, I found a package of contraceptive inserts in the hall closet. My guess is that they fell out of something."

"Were any missing?"

"No."

"Did you initiate a discussion on birth control with Andi?"

"I wouldn't know where to begin," answered Ed, unsettled by Zemmel's approach.

"Why didn't you talk to Sarah?"

"I didn't want to upset her. She and Andi were having a rough time.

"Mm," said Zemmel, bridging his fingers together, "sounds like a lot of question marks."

"Questions are easier than answers", observed Ed slowly. "I saw myself as trying to protect everyone."

"What about protecting yourself?"

"From them?"

"No, I was thinking more in terms of protecting yourself from your own feelings. By not confronting your wife and daughter, you also avoided yourself."

"Your point on confrontation is well taken."

"How so?"

"From Andi's first date with Joe, my wife started to complain that he wasn't Jewish. I also want Andi to marry someone who's Jewish, but she's only sixteen and I don't see the necessity for all this pressure. Yet I never brought it up. Like you said, I didn't want to get into a hassle."

He paused and Zemmel motioned for him to continue.

"I'm positive my wife and I handled things very poorly, when the boy broke off with Andi. She needed support that we obviously didn't give."

"You seem disappointed with Sarah."

"I allowed Sarah to take the lead even though I didn't totally agree with her philosophy."

"And now you're rethinking things."

"Mm, I sure let things slip with Andi. I never confronted the depth of her feelings. It was easier to keep thinking of her as a little kid. I acted like the boy was just a phase. She really hated both of us for that."

"Will your new thoughts about Andi create a conflict in your relationship with Sarah?"

"Obviously I've got to let Sarah know how I feel. We may argue about Andi, but I have to take the risk. Sarah would be happy if Andi never spoke to Joe again. But I see it differently. By the way, why can't you let her talk to him? I understand he's been calling Andi."

"He has, but he could do her more harm than good."

"What's so good about this place? My daughter's thin as a rail, almost raped and about to have a second nervous breakdown over a phone call."

107

"Are you sure this isn't your guilt speaking?"

"That's a cheap shot."

"It seems to me that your daughter's been voicing one long scream for help," said Zemmel carefully. "For instance, anyone who's actually using birth control and concealing it from her parents, wouldn't leave the whole package in a hall closet."

"Do you think Andi wanted us to discover the inserts and confront her with them?"

"I think she wanted to talk about her feelings."

"And we ignored her."

"When you remained aloof, she probably tried other methods."

"Such as the suicide attempt?"

"That was probably her most drastic effort. Andi obviously has a very urgent need to talk about herself; her feelings are very intense."

"Well, if talking's so important for her, why can't she talk to Joe?" asked Ed.

"Here, we regulate the dialogue so anxiety is minimal. But a conversation with Joe could destabilize the delicate balance we've created and produce negative repercussions."

"I assume you're talking about a panic attack."

"Correct."

"You make a good case, but Andi's heart is set on talking with this guy and I don't see that one conversation with him will undo all your therapy. Frankly, she's already building up like a pressure cooker, and I'm afraid of another explosion."

"I'm sensing a lot of pressure in you this morning," observed Zemmel.

"Don't play Freud with me, Zemmel," snapped Ed angrily.

"I'm not playing; it's my profession."

"Look, you may be a shrink, but I'm not a patient. I merely came here out of concern for my daughter, not to get my head shrunk."

"I realize that, but this is all part of the process."

"What process?"

"A family trying to rebuild. I've seen much anger in Andi and now I'm seeing it in you," said Zemmel in a conciliatory tone.

"I suppose that translates into I'm supposed to sit here and spill my guts."

"If that's what it takes. But not this visit. Your hour is almost up."

"You mean my 45 minutes."

"True."

"I never pictured myself in therapy," said Ed.

"People rarely do, but it often helps unlock hidden resources."

"What about Andi and her phone call? She asked me to speak with you and now she'll think I just ignored her."

"I'll handle it. Call me tomorrow morning."

Ed visibly relaxed. Talking to this guy was better than I thought, he told himself, and attempted his first humor in weeks, "Kind of like take two aspirins and call me in the morning?"

"Yeah," laughed Zemmel, "but I'm the one with the headache."

CHAPTER 19

"Sandi, you have an emergency phone call. It's your daughter," said an orderly to Ms. Glover.

"Oh, gosh, my daughter...could you watch the kids till I get back?"

"Well uh..."

"There are only six of them."

"O.K., I guess I can handle it," Jim agreed.

"Thanks," said Sandi and left.

"O.K., kids, just keep doing whatever you're doing," announced the orderly in good humor, and took a novel out of his back pocket. Tina mysteriously pulled several pairs of doctor's gloves from her notebook, "Psst, Yolanda. Pass these around. Let's give that guy a scare."

"Mm," said Mouth, "what do you have in mind?"

There's that strange voice again, thought Andi. Where'd he come from?

"Who's he?" asked Yolanda.

"A real whack," whispered Tina. "They don't even let him in this class most of the time."

"Listen bitch, I'm talking to you," hissed the boy.

"Oh yeah, Mouth? Why don't you just shut up?" said Tina.

"Make me!" challenged the short, mildly deformed boy.

"I've got something in my sock that'll make you shit, so back off," Tina warned.

Her stinging words baited him and he couldn't let them pass. If there was something in her sock, he would make it his. Without another thought, the short boy rushed at Tina like a pit bull. But she was too quick for him, and deftly pulled out one of the five vials of blood hidden in her sock.

"You want what I have?" she asked serenely, opening the rubber stopper.

The orderly looked up from his book and his mouth dropped open in disbelief. The small boy's hair was dripping with blood.

Time froze for Andi. Her worst nightmare stared her in the face. And she embraced it. She wanted the blood. Red magic markers weren't good enough to draw Danny anymore. She needed real blood to depict the horror.

Andi took a paintbrush from Ms. Glover's desk. "I want that blood, Tina. Let me have some."

No, thought the orderly, this can't be happening. He knew he should act. He should summon Sandi Glover. But he couldn't move. He couldn't believe his eyes. Now they were drawing with blood all over the room. Even the short boy with the bloody hair they called Mouth—especially Mouth! In fact, he was drawing a mouth—a huge mouth with thick lips framing teeth that dripped red. Underneath the mouth blared the words, *Put it there Baby*, in garish clotted red.

Yolanda looked at Mouth with new respect, "You really can draw."

"Watch this," he answered with a flourish, glad of an audience. "Here's something to go with it," he announced and deftly outlined an obscenely large pair of woman's breasts. "Tits," he said proudly.

The walls of the room were quickly smeared with blood. Plastic gloves turned red and the room stank. But the tension was gone and there was camaraderie in its place.

"Where the hell's Glover," Jim muttered to himself. "She ain't gonna pin this on me."

"I didn't know you had so little respect for this room," came Ms. Glover's deep voice.

"I'm outta here," intoned Jim and left.

No one else said a word.

"What can you expect from mental patients?" Carlos eventually offered.

"We are nuts," Mouth agreed proudly.

"Speak for yourself," hissed Yolanda.

"You're definitely going back to the psycho ward, Mouth," commented Tina.

"Et tu Brutus," Mouth replied mockingly, and gave Tina the finger from within his blood-stained plastic glove.

Andi looked from his hands to his face. His left cheek was sunken and one eye teared. He was extremely ugly. "Why are you so gross," she blurted.

"Where do you think you are?" Ms. Glover finally managed to assert herself, still shaken by the news of her daughter's car accident.

"We're in a loony bin, Lady," smirked Mouth.

Mouth's disruptive behavior usually grated on Ms. Glover, but today she was more vulnerable to his attack and he completely unnerved her.

"This is a hospital," she said with a hostile edge in her voice, "and you are a patient."

"And you're losing it," prompted the short boy.

"Maybe you're right," said Ms. Glover in louder tones, actually sickened by the bloodied walls. "Maybe I am a failure. You've finally convinced me that you're incurable."

Carlos suddenly developed hiccups. It was hard for him to see his stalwart teacher so weakened. The noise caught Ms. Glover's attention, and she turned to the group at large. "Don't you have any respect for me or this room or yourselves," she demanded in a cracking voice. This room is for you; not me. I always thought you considered it a bright spot in this drab place. But I guess it never meant that much to you, and in five minutes you've desecrated what we've built together each and every day."

There was no response, but she knew they were listening and that gave her strength to continue. "It's true you're here because you have problems. But you know right from wrong, and what you did was wrong. When you defiled this room, you defiled me and yourselves."

"Maybe that's why we're here," said Andi softly. "Because we're defiled."

"You're a loon," jeered Mouth.

"We're here to start cleaning ourselves up," continued Andi, purposely ignoring him.

"Well then, start with this mess," declared Ms. Glover with hope that wouldn't quit. "Grab some buckets and sponges from the back closet. And Marvin..."

"Call me Mouth," he interrupted.

"Fine," she agreed. "It suits you only too well...Mouth, wash your head out in the sink."

"You'll never get that slime ball to use soap," remarked Tina.

"Lay off him," said Yolanda. "I once knew someone that looked like him. He had a stroke."

"Just don't touch my picture," whined Jerry.

"What's so special about it?" asked Tina filling up her bucket.

"Nothing, but it's my tree," said Jerry.

"Boy, this stuff really washes off easily," said Carlos, scrubbing his picture of a bright red fire engine.

"I don't think you can ever really wash blood away," said Andi thoughtfully. "You may think it's gone, but it's still there."

"Really? You're washing your picture of Danny away," countered Yolanda.

"It may be off the wall, but it's not out of my mind. Just like I can't forget about the blood in my room."

And then she glanced down at her hands. They were sweating under the red stained plastic gloves. "See my hands, Yolanda. They're all bloody like the night I cut myself cause I thought Joe betrayed me. It's just like the blood never left, even though I washed my hands."

"Andi," laughed Yolanda nervously, "you're sending goose bumps up my spine."

Andi's voice was almost trance-like when she finally said," I thought I tried to kill myself because of Joe, but now I'm not so sure. I don't know how much he really matters to me."

"You always say Joe's so important," interrupted Yolanda. "What's changed?"

"Maybe I have," answered Andi.

"Hey guys, she's a real Lady Macbeth," jeered Mouth.

Andi turned as red as the blood. They were all staring at her. What's really important to me, she wondered. She wanted to say how confused she was feeling, but she didn't dare. Everyone would just laugh, and she couldn't bear the humiliation.

"Are you mad at me, Andi?" asked Yolanda, mistaking her friend's confusion for being insulted.

"I believe Andi's just letting us know that she went through enough for one day," interjected Ms. Glover.

"At least she didn't get electric shocked," commented Jerry.

"She looks like she needs some," remarked Mouth.

"Shut up you idiot," said Yolanda, feeling protective of Andi.

"Shut up yourself, fat-stuff, or you might wind up in the electric chair," smirked Mouth.

"Look Mouth, I know you had a stroke and on top of that, you ain't all there. But get this straight, I don't take shit." With those words, Yolanda threw her bucket of water in his face.

"Mouth finally got a bath," laughed Jerry.

Suddenly, they were all laughing; even Ms. Glover and Mouth.

"Bet you thought we'd never get this place clean, Ms. Glover," said Carlos.

"You've got that backwards, Carlos. I never dreamed you'd bloody up these walls in the first place. By the way, how'd that blood get in here, anyway?"

Tina was just cleaning off the tip of the stiletto she'd drawn, and didn't say a word. Neither did anyone else.

"Mm, for once there's silence," said Ms. Glover.

"I kind of like the quiet," said Andi.

"Well, I know the blood didn't just walk in by itself," coaxed Ms. Glover.

"Even we know that," answered Jerry.

Again, there was only silence.

"Your tree looks really lonely, Jerry, now that the other pictures are gone," observed Andi.

"Maybe I should wash it off after all," he answered.

"Maybe you should," exclaimed Ms. Glover, glad of a rational thought.

"But it was kinda neat," said Andi, smiling.

"So are you," Jerry answered, and smiled back.

CHAPTER 20

Andi entered Dr. Zemmel's office in a state of confusion. Since class, her feelings about Joe were unclear. Her mind kept flashing back to the bloody plastic gloves and her slashed wrists. Could she ever make the blood disappear? She sat down, but was bewildered about where to begin. She looked to Zemmel for direction and got the usual stare.

Zemmel watched Andi enter and he free associated to the black-hatted Yeshiva student, Chaim Katz. Zemmel was intrigued by abstract spirituality, but he relegated religious practice to the furthest corners of obscurity. The memory of the ritualistically dressed student collecting charity challenged Zemmel's point of view. He recognized a commitment and faith that he rarely encountered; a reality he didn't comprehend.

"Dr. Zemmel," said Andi expectantly.

The girl's voice jarred Zemmel. He suppressed his thoughts and focused on her. He recalled his recent visit with her father and was certain of a tough session. Gradually, he relaxed into the familiar doctor/patient relationship and he stared at her with genuine interest.

"I don't know what to say," she finally began. "Everything's different. I think it's because of the class."

"Perhaps you're starting to build relationships in the class."

"Kind of...but it's confusing."

"Doesn't it feel good to have friends?"

"Yeah..." said Andi uncertainly.

"How is it confusing?"

"Up until today, I thought my problems centered around Joe, but now I'm not so sure."

"Why not?"

"We were drawing graffiti in class this morning. I drew Danny. Later I washed the picture off the wall and it came out really easily. But at the same time, I knew that I wasn't getting him out of my mind even though the picture was fading.

"The picture on the wall was fading, but you were focusing on something else," said Zemmel sharply. "What was it?"

"I wondered if one day the hate would leave. And then I thought about my ache for Joe and I hoped that I wouldn't have to carry it forever. And that feeling was different."

"It was different because you're gaining strength. You realize you have a choice about your ache and the amount of pain you choose to carry with you."

"You're right. Up until this morning, I enjoyed my ache even though it hurt. I always kept it next to me. It was the most important thing in my life. Without it, my life was meaningless. But now I'm wondering why my life's been so meaningless. Why do I want to go around feeling bad? Will I ever be able to feel anything without Joe?"

Her last words were almost a tearful whisper. Zemmel was pleased with her progress and gently urged her forward. "You're telling me that Joe was not only a boyfriend. He was a way of stating who you are, and you're not sure how you'll be able to define yourself without him." Andi nodded and Zemmel continued, "What feelings did you connect with Joe? Why did it feel good to be with him?"

"I never felt lonely with him," she answered quietly.

"And without him?"

"There was a fright, kind of like when you wake up from a nightmare."

"So, what's the connection between Joe and the nightmarish, frightened feelings."

"When I was with him, I didn't have those feelings! But when he left..."

"Go on," Zemmel encouraged her.

"When I heard he was going out with someone else, those terrible feelings started closing in on me and...and...I..."

Zemmel guessed where she was headed, and purposely did not supply her with words when she faltered. He trusted they would come eventually. Rather, he steered her away from the absolute edge of her trauma in order to explore her anxiety further. "Let's back up and try to define the loneliness and why you found it so frightening."

"I have no words for it," she answered softly, aware they were on safer ground.

"Search for them. Picture yourself lonely."

"Why are you talking so much?"

"Because I think you're ready."

"For what?"

"To start making some sense of your life, and talk about what it's like to grow up into a healthy young woman."

"I guess I first started feeling lonely when I got unbelievably frantic over almost anything."

"How so?"

"Never wanting to stay home, arguing with my mother constantly, hating my name."

"Why do you hate your name?"

"The name Andrea just sounds so old fashioned. It's too nerdy for me. Besides, it was her idea and I need to cut myself..."

"Why did you stop so suddenly?" asked Zemmel after a few moments. "What happened?"

"When I said the word 'cut', it reminded me of the blood."

"The blood when you cut yourself?"

"Mm. Today we were drawing with blood. Someone brought it to class. Even though I was wearing plastic gloves, my hands looked bloody. It made me feel like I could never get rid of the blood from the night I slashed my wrists."

Once again Zemmel pictured the Yeshiva student, Chaim Katz. But this time his white shirt and *tzitzit* were covered with blood. Jews can never get away from blood, he thought.

And then he saw Andi's hands. They looked clean to him, but were apparently defiled to her. "It's true Andi, we can't just wash away bad feelings. Let's go back to your name. Why does it hurt you so much?"

"I was saying I needed to cut myself off from my mother. She gave me the name, so I hated it."

"Are you sure it's the name that you hate?"

"You make it sound like it's really my mother...well you're right." She always said she loved me, but she could never accept me for myself. She even wanted to take away the one person I loved...Joe. Joe understands me and my mother never will."

"What does he understand about you?"

"He understands my feelings."

"Tell us about that."

"Just before Joe and I stopped seeing each other, supposedly temporarily, he kept telling me to slow down. He knew how unhappy and out of control I felt. But I couldn't concentrate on anything he said. All I did was cry."

"Why?"

"I cried because I let him see me naked."

"Wasn't it good for you?"

"Yes, I felt very close..."

"So why the tears?"

"I wanted that closeness all the time, but he didn't. He said I was too dependent on him and he didn't want me clinging to him. We started arguing about when to see each other and it made me cry. Joe hated my tears. He said I used them as a weapon. Do you think that's true?"

"I'm not sure. Tell me more."

"He started pulling away from me right after we got really close. I thought he didn't like me."

"Perhaps your intensity frightened him."

"Maybe, but I thought it was because I looked ugly."

"I think he recognized your softness, but he wasn't ready to share it with you. He didn't feel equal to your femininity."

"Do you think Joe saw me as a woman?"

"Very possibly. But he didn't know what to do about it, so he withdrew."

"I can't picture anyone seeing me as a woman."

"Why not?

"I'm pretty skinny right now and my breasts are too small. My mother's are large."

"Does that bother you?"

"I'm not sure. It might. That's part of why I never seem grown up in my family."

"But you had some pretty grown up feelings with Joe, didn't you?"

"At first he made me feel very attractive. But when he pulled away, those feelings disappeared. At home it was even worse."

"How so?"

"When I came home after being with Joe, my mother treated me like a criminal."

"Why?"

"Because he wasn't Jewish."

"Your arguments seem to center around your mother's ideas rather than your feelings."

"I guess because she strongly believes in G-d, and I'm not sure I do. By the way, isn't my hour up yet?"

"Not quite; don't avoid me. How do you feel about not being allowed to form your own opinions?"

"I feel like a two year old. How should I feel? No one cares about what I think. You certainly don't or you'd let me talk to Joe. I bet my father never even spoke to you about that."

"He did, but let's not lose track of this discussion. It's important. This is a valid aspect of the decision making process. Before we can take action, we need to understand your feelings."

"I just told you how I feel—like a baby."

"I hear that as anger for your mother."

"I want my mother to trust me—to have faith in me."

"That sounds like the beginning of your own voice; not colored by anyone else's thinking. Speak to her directly."

"See me the way I am, not the way you want me to appear. I'm not a baby. Let me make my own decisions—my own mistakes."

"How would she respond?"

"I don't want you to get hurt Andi."

"Answer her."

"It's O.K. Ma. I'm already hurt."

"Tell her about the hurt."

"I want you to love me where I'm soft. But you don't see me there. I'm invisible to you and that hurts."

"What's it like to be invisible?"

"Like I don't exist."

"I don't think you were invisible to Joe. He saw you."

"Yes, but he didn't want my love. Now I'm stuck with a lot of feeling with no place to put it."

"Bring it here—into your therapy."

"Why should I? This is only an office; not a place for love."

"Isn't this a place for feeling? Isn't love a feeling?"

"Maybe..."

"Let's hold that thought for tomorrow."

"I don't want to. First you tell me to bring my love here and then you tell me to leave."

"Love encompasses very intense feelings. We need to explore them slowly and with caution."

Andi's breathing accelerated. "I'm choking! I can't leave!"

"Relax Andi. That's one of your panic symptoms. Regulate your breathing. You'll be fine."

"Maybe I don't want to be," she muttered, but she adjusted her breathing pattern.

"Better?" he asked.

"Not really," she answered and knew she was lying.

121

So did he.

Suddenly, she felt grown up with Dr. Zemmel and smiled. "I guess I've had enough for one day," she said, and walked out the door.

CHAPTER 21

Bliss felt she was suspended between worlds of light and darkness, as she climbed the steps from the subway into the late afternoon sun. She enjoyed hurtling in the dark anonymity of tunnels and whizzing through dimly lit stations. In the street, the sunlight threatened her.

Marty was coming for dinner, and she was ashamed to let Adam know about him. How can you be an effective role model to an impressionable 15 year old when you're seeing a married man, she questioned herself harshly.

Grow up, came a quick reply. His friends' mothers are probably doing the same thing. In any event, Adam's spending the night out—relax.

Yet her mind still raced as she turned the last corner before her apartment building. You've got to let Marty go, she admonished herself.

I'm not ready to, so forget it. Let me enjoy life for once. Why the hell did I get a divorce, she continued her inner dialogue and walked inside the building.

In the elevator, she recalled the yeshiva student, Chaim Katz, and her torment continued. His black hat and white shirt reminded her of her childhood. Bliss attended yeshiva till the sixth grade and her ideas were still colored by traditional Judaism. The question she tackled when she stepped from the elevator was whether her relationship with Marty was good or evil. She saw no compromise.

I met him by chance, she said to herself, so it was *beshert*. I can't avoid my destiny.

What about free choice? If you met a bum in the park that afternoon, would you call that *beshert*, she answered herself and unlocked the door to her apartment.

But I didn't meet a bum. I met Marty and he's good for me. G-d put him there for me, she argued and sank into a kitchen chair.

Really? Since when did G-d become a home wrecker. Can't you take any responsibility for your actions?

Bliss pictured Marty's wife and wondered if she suspected his adultery. Am I really to blame, she asked herself.

This isn't the Middle Ages and other people's bad marriages aren't my concern, retorted Bliss and kicked off her shoes.

Don't act so aloof. It's wrong and you know it, Bliss finally answered herself and started to wash last night's dishes.

Although Bliss rebelled against the traditional world of her parents, she could never escape it. She was always haunted by the old parameters. Her attempts to shape a world were ultimately thwarted by a series of rights and wrongs she could never quite accept or reject. At best, she compromised by living in two worlds. But mostly, she lived in loneliness.

And now there's Marty, she mused. How can anything that feels so good be wrong?

When it's evil, she thought, spotting the pamphlets that Chaim Katz left. Just because you met him, didn't mean you had to pursue a relationship.

But aren't coincidences from G-d, she pleaded with herself. So is free choice, she noted, and picked up the pamphlet entitled, Insights into Levels of Jewish Mysticism. She conjectured about how many levels of mysticism there might be and glanced at the table of contents. Bliss was immediately struck by the words, "Souls Calling Souls." Everything suddenly appeared tightly interwoven; the way she met Marty, the way he seemed so perfect for her, yet wasn't, and the way that student popped into her life and gave her literature with fascinating language that seemed somehow alive..."Souls Calling Souls."

Yes, she agreed. Something is calling me. But what is it? I feel like I'm missing the point, or maybe I'm being used in some weird cosmic experiment. As she continued to skim the

Contents, she noticed a chapter on prayer and recalled her own yeshiva days.

The teachers used to enforce prayer every morning and Bliss hated the meaningless ritual. So, she moved her lips, but said nothing. Not only did her prayers go unanswered, but she remained the slowest reader in the class.

But now, Bliss's perspective was drastically different from grammar school. She was 38 and a single parent. Perhaps there are hidden elements to life, she speculated, and began to leaf through the pages of the booklet until she noticed the word, "sin"..."Sin can be cloaked according to our tastes, our mood, etc. It can make itself completely compatible with our psyche." Chilled, she saw an answer to her question concerning Marty. "Evil can become exactly what you want it to be," she read out loud. Reading further, she was confronted with an affirmation of her earlier thinking, "While situations are decreed, our reactions are not..."

So this isn't my imagination. It's the real thing—sin, Bliss concluded. That's why Marty seems so perfect, she thought cynically. He's absolutely tailored to my needs. This is more complex than I thought, she almost said aloud, as she prepared a rice and bean dish for the dinner she promised Marty that evening. Bliss added rice to boiling water and considered her responsibility to choose between her body and her soul, but it was too painful. I'm not ready for this, she decided. These guys don't talk about fun. Who knows? Maybe sin's not really so bad once you understand it, she told herself, and tossed the pamphlet onto the kitchen counter.

Where's Marty anyway, she worried, peeling and then dicing the onions. I hope my punishment's not starting already. Thoughts of good and evil still nagged at her and, while she waited for the onions, carrots, mushrooms and peppers to saute, she opened the pamphlet again. This time she flipped to the end. "We all have an ache for Hashem or G-d," she read. True, I sure have an ache, but how do I know it's for Hashem. Convinced her ache was for her lover, she set the table and dimmed the lights.

CHAPTER 22

The dining area was unusually quiet that evening as Andi joined Yolanda and Tina. Andi pushed away the hamburger and nibbled at the canned peas and carrots. The conversation sounded meaningless. It was difficult to delve into herself in therapy only to be thrown back into the mundane world of small talk. Andi still didn't know how to balance the two worlds. She was drained from therapy and wanted everyone to leave her alone. Earlier, she had begged Mary for permission to eat by her cot.

"Oh Andi," said Tina, "it's all arranged. You're on for next week."

Andi literally didn't know how to respond. Tina sensed her dilemma and elaborated, "Are you in a trance? I'm talking about Joe. I told you I was going to arrange things."

Andi's stomach sank. "I've been rethinking things, Tina. I tried to tell you that the other day."

"But what about me and all I've done?" complained Tina.

"What exactly have you done?" questioned Yolanda.

"Oh forget it. I guess I went off the deep end going into other peoples' business."

While they discussed her, a germ of an idea took root in Andi. Maybe this isn't so bad after all, she thought. If Joe's really so intent on seeing me, this might be the perfect opportunity for me to reject him. The more she considered ways to hurt Joe, the calmer she grew. Revenge might even dull the pain of the daily psychosurgery in Dr. Zemmel's office. For once, she gloated inwardly, I'll be in control.

"Hold it Tina," she smiled sweetly, "I'm sorry for being out of it. You're right; we did agree. But what about her?" she glanced back at Mary. "Remember, I'm still under surveillance."

"That's the one hitch," said Tina. "You've got to gain independence. How's your therapy going?"

Getting dreamy again, Andi whispered, "Good."

"Zombie Land," commented Yolanda.

Wrapped up in her inner world, Andi continued in stream of consciousness. "When Dr. Zemmel and I really get into my feelings, it's like the whole world is gone and it's only us. All that matters is what I think and feel. I love it and I never want our sessions to end. But when they do, I just want to lie around thinking and feeling some more. I just don't care about anything."

"Sounds like you're worse now than when I first met you!" said Yolanda.

"I know what Andi means," said Tina sympathetically, "I've always been into my feelings. When you're not used to it, I guess it can be kind of earth shattering."

"I'll tell you one thing," retorted Yolanda, "whatever she's talkin' about, I ain't plannin' on gettin' used to it."

"Look kid," Tina directed herself to Andi, ignoring Yolanda's remarks, "you've got to snap out of it. Remember, we're gonna party."

"Now you got it," agreed Yolanda.

At the mention of the word "party", Andi crashed down to earth with a heavy thump. What am I thinking about, she wondered to herself. I'm a complete wreck. My clothes are huge and baggy 'cause I lost so much weight. Besides, I don't have anything decent to wear anyway. Joe will just think I'm some kind of freak.

"Tina, this is all a mistake," Andi finally said out loud. "I have nothing to wear. Nobody would want me."

"Andi, relax," cajoled Tina, "I've got tons of clothes and I may even be thinner than you. Come try them on. I promise to be honest about the way you look."

"I'd offer you my clothes, joked Yolanda, "but you know they'd never fit."

"How am I going to get rid of Mary, then," asked Andi, determined to voice all her objections. "Especially when I don't really want to. I like her a lot."

"We thought you hated jail," both girls quickly retorted.

"I do, but I like Mary and I need her. She's very important after I see my shrink."

Tina was impatient, "Look Andi, you're either with this thing or you're not—there's no middle ground."

"It's not that simple," protested Andi. You're acting like we're in some damn boarding school trying to sneak in guys. This is a hospital, Tina, and my goal is to get better. I'm starting to see myself for the first time ever, and I like it. My work with Dr. Zemmel is much better than I thought possible and I don't want to destroy it."

"You still need friends, don't you?" said Yolanda, privately moved by Andi's admission.

"Yes, but sometimes friends can pressure you to be someone you're not."

"Is that the way you think of us?" asked Tina, with a very hurt expression.

"No, Tina, of course not," said Andi, not wanting to hurt Tina's feelings, "you've been so kind to me I can't even figure out why you're here."

"I hate to admit it, but I function much better in here than outside. The truth is I'm afraid to leave."

"Boy, I sure hope that doesn't happen to me," said Yolanda very soberly. "Like Andi said, it's better than I thought here. Ms. Glover's the best teacher there is and you two may be the best friends I ever had. But this is still a bug house and I want to get out."

"Thanks Bubba, I appreciate that," said Tina. "We really are good friends, aren't we. But let's stick to business, guys. Andi, I'm gonna make you gorgeous. This guy's gonna drool for you. Deal?"

"Since you put it that way...deal," agreed Andi.

"But you've got to get that nurse out. The whole plan hinges on it," urged Tina.

"I'll do my best, but what about the clothes. Oh G-d, I'm so sick of these ugly rags. My mother's taste is really the pits."

"First dessert," said Tina, reaching for the pie.

"Are you sure you're gonna make me look good?"

"Positive!"

"It's super important. I want Joe to die for me. I want him to lose himself because of me."

"While you keep control," surmised Yolanda.

"I get it now," said Tina, "you wanna bust this guy."

"That's right," smirked Andi, "and I'm counting on you."

"Andi, does it still hurt that much?" asked Tina.

"Maybe not all the time—but enough."

"But you said Joe might not be such a great part of your misery," suggested Tina. "Can't you guys at least be friends? He sure sounds nice on the phone."

"Look Tina, stop playing shrink. But since you mentioned it, I know I was a fool about a lot of things. You're right! Joe might not be the total cause of my problems. But he really let me down when I needed him. Actually, I think it's a sign of health that I'm not crawling back for more."

"And is revenge also a sign of health?" inquired Tina sarcastically.

"Maybe it is," declared Andi heatedly.

"Calm down you two," laughed Yolanda, "and take my advice. You know what I'd do—just beat the shit outta that guy and go on to the next one."

"What about the clothes?" asked Andi, trying to change the subject.

"What about your nurse," countered Tina, feeling strangely cheated out of leadership.

"Don't worry about her. This evening, she actually begged me to eat with you two...now they're afraid I'm too introverted."

*   *   *   *

Trailing the girls to Tina's private room, Mary was glad Andi was talking and laughing with the others. Not wanting to intimidate the trio, the nurse hung in the background; far enough to respect privacy, but close enough to detect trouble. Everything looks innocent enough, she reassured herself.

Inside the room, Yolanda and Andi grew wide eyed at Tina's collection. Sequins, glitter, satin, plunging backs, mini skirts, bare midriffs and low necklines sure jazzed up the dreary green of the place.

"My mother would die if she even saw me looking at this stuff," gasped Andi.

"You sure you don't work in the city somewhere?" joked Yolanda pointedly.

"I don't actually wear any of this much, Tina replied evenly without taking offense. Rather, I collect it for my fantasy life."

Afraid to speculate on that fantasy life, the girls said nothing.

"What are you waiting for? Dig in," invited Tina. "Don't worry about your mother, Andi. Just use your imagination."

Knowing she would never wear it in public, Andi selected a green spaghetti strapped gown, and was astounded at how attractive her thin figure looked in Tina's full length mirror.

"What about this?" asked Tina, offering her a ruffled mini-skirt with a matching short top.

"O.K."

"Hey look at you," admired Tina, "you look better already."

"She does look kinda cute," assented Yolanda.

Andi was buoyed by their support and turned to her friends in confidence. "I've never worn anything this sexy before...but what if Joe doesn't like it?"

The tension of the moment reached Mary`s intuition. Glad for her antenna, the nurse unobtrusively moved closer.

"Are you worried about Joe or are you worried about your mother?" intoned Tina with her usual perception.

"I guess I am worried about her. She always tried to baby me. She couldn't bear for me to have a life of my own."

"What do you mean?"

"When I met Joe, she really got on my case. Once I got in a few minutes after my curfew and she grounded me for a week. I really started to hate her. It's like she wanted to live her life through me and, when my life didn't go according to her fantasies, she lost it."

"Maybe she was afraid you were having sex," said Yolanda.

"No, I don't think so. She always thinks of me as her little baby."

"Forget your mother. What about you and Joe?" urged Yolanda anxiously.

But Andi couldn't stop focusing on her mother. "When she figured Joe and I broke up, she was so happy, she actually gloated to her friends. One day I overheard her talking on the phone. She said I was just going through a phase, thank G-d!"

It was definitely time for Mary to interrupt. Sure she'd let things go too long, Mary was quietly firm with Andi. "Come on Andi, I thought you wanted a quiet night. It's time to go."

"Andi, we want to know about Joe; not your mother," Tina interjected.

Secretly grateful for the interruption, Andi ignored her friend's curiosity, "Gotta go. Thanks for everything."

The walk back to the cot soothed Andi's nerves, and she was able to smooth over the jagged edges that felt razor sharp in Tina's room.

"I guess I made my mother sound like an ogre back there," Andi confided to Mary. "A lot of the time my mother and I overreact to each other. Whenever we discuss things, she never allows me to make my own decisions. It's like everything I say is wrong. That's what I hate. She doesn't give me breathing space."

"Some families tend to get over intense. Perhaps yours is one of them," Mary answered carefully.

"Mary, I like you a lot, but I resent a 24-hour watch. How long does this go on?"

"It goes on until you are secure enough to make choices that are positive rather than self-destructive."

"Who's the judge of that?" questioned Andi testily.

Mary smiled into her patient's frown. "Cheer up Andi. You're really making much progress in the right direction."

"Even though I'm not completely happy about certain things in my life, I want to be in charge of myself. I'm not running anymore. Death doesn't tempt me. I know that I want to live more now than I did a week ago."

Andi relaxed when the hospital lights dimmed. For once, she was glad to go to bed. What she said to Mary was true. She was much more involved with life now, but she needed the quietness. All the little decisions that went into living were becoming relevant again. Life was not just an amorphous dullness with no future other than an ache. She could give shape to things. She just wasn't sure what those shapes should be. I'm not ready for big decisions yet, she told herself. Let me stick to little ones right now—like going to bed. I'm not going to bed because of the curfew. I'm going because I'm tired. She hoped this was one decision in a series that would enable her to gain independence.

CHAPTER 23

Psychotherapy was something Ed Levy never envisioned for himself. He was an attorney for a very active law firm that specialized in real estate. His view of his work was pragmatic and his clients were generally predictable to him. Although his private life was in shambles, in the office he was considered a highly skilled communicator, who could always maintain balance in the most delicate situations. Everything had its place and he knew what it was. Whatever didn't fit the pattern could easily be shifted.

And then this thing happened with Andi. But it wasn't just a thing and it didn't just happen, he chided himself sitting in Dr. Zemmel's waiting room. Peering at himself with prowess he usually reserved for the courtroom, he admitted his family's problems were developing for years. However, thanks to his daughter, it was out in the open and he needed to determine his responsibility. Otherwise, he believed the guilty feeling in his gut would last forever. Every morning it was there when he woke up, and he hated it. The thought of that terrified him more than sitting across from the shrink. As much as Levy desired to see his daughter, he was grateful that Zemmel maintained an office apart from the hospital. This place was a lot less intimidating. But where was Zemmel? There was a strangely vacant air in the waiting room. Levy was almost positive that there was no one behind Zemmel's door. He felt anxious waiting to spill his guts, unsure if he would actually get the opportunity.

"Hi Ed," said Zemmel, coming through the street door, "Sorry I'm late." Ed followed Zemmel into the office and his mind blanked suddenly. He wondered what he was doing there.

They stared at each other over a short space of beige carpeting. Zemmel smiled blandly and popped a cough drop. He believed it was better to say nothing than to prove himself inane. So he remained silent, and for an instant he pictured the wine he'd just bought for Bliss.

Pressured to set the agenda, Levy studied the carpeting and noticed some stains. "How do I know you're right for me?" he asked.

"I thought we had decent rapport on your last visit," answered Zemmel.

"But you're Andi's doctor. Do you do family therapy?"

"Mm hmm."

"Well I don't go for this silent treatment. I'll be honest. I'm stumped."

"Take your time. It'll come."

"I never thought I would be in a place like this seeing someone like you. This seems like something my wife would do."

"Does she see anyone?"

"No."

"Hmm."

"But she's very introspective."

"Tell me more about your wife."

"She's really into herself. Lately, she's become more religious."

"How does that affect you?"

"Truthfully, I ignore a lot of it."

"Is that the way you generally cope with personal problems?"

"Sounds pretty awful hearing you put it that way, Doctor. But I guess I've indulged in tuning out quite a bit. With some of the rapid-fire changes in my home, I admittedly don't always know how to react."

"Thanks for your honesty. In our last session, we also talked about communication problems."

"I'm glad you mentioned that. It's not the same for Sarah and me anymore."

"How so?"

"We lead separate lives. There's little intimacy. We only talk about practical matters; the house, Andi, my career, bills, etc. What I mean is there's no romance left."

"Breathe life into the romance you're missing. Make it real for now."

"Look, this is embarrassing for me. Usually women talk about these things."

"By things, you mean feelings."

"Right, it's the old thing. Men are supposed to be strong, the protectors. And I guess I'm not good enough."

"You're very hard on yourself."

Well, look at me. My daughter's in the hospital and I'm sitting here talking about myself."

"Downing yourself really doesn't work. However, repairing your marriage with Sarah might help heal everyone's problems. Interestingly, women are often more attuned to feelings than men. But it certainly doesn't make you less of a man to be the partner to express sensitivity and a desire for more."

"Well, should I bring Sarah in next time?"

"I don't think we need to decide that right now. Let's go back a few steps to your need for romance. Tell me about it."

"I want to feel passionate again. I know it's still there, but the romance is clouded by problems."

"Forget the problems. Focus on the love."

"Like being impulsive. Going to our favorite pond. Just us—alone—swimming naked. There's no fun anymore and that bothers me."

"Does it bother Sarah?"

"I'm not sure she wants that anymore. She's changed. I haven't."

"Is there any common ground between the two of you?"

"If there is, it's well hidden."

"Maybe you'll have to create new ground which includes some of her new ideas."

"I've never taken her new ideas seriously."

"Her ideas may be tied in with her love."

"Hmm, I was so busy trying to avoid arguments that I never stopped to consider other possibilities."

"I thought attorneys enjoy confrontation."

"In the courtroom, yes; at home, no."

"What about your risk taking side? Why are you so tame with Sarah?"

"I put my aggression into my career."

"Sounds like you need some reorganization in your management style. You may be the one that shifted the passion right out of your marriage."

"When Sarah started to make decisions on her own, I felt threatened."

"Did you ever bother to enter the ring?"

"No, I ran back to the office where they played the game the way I played it."

"That assured you of a clear win."

"Correct...Maybe that's why I feel all this guilt. Sarah needed my brain at home. Instead, I gave her a reasonable facsimile."

"It's certainly not too late to take action. Andi's doing well, but she's going to need a lot of strength from you and Sarah. There's plenty of room for you to grow as a family."

"No way to go but up, huh?"

"Seriously, you seem committed to developing a more compatible relationship with your wife. Together, you can start making intelligent adjustments in your lifestyles. But Andi's got to be included. She needs her ideas to be recognized and accepted."

"Dr. Zemmel, your advice is well taken. I'm under a tremendous amount of stress and this session's been helpful."

"Glad to hear it. I'll reserve the same time for next week. Would you like to bring Sarah?"

"Yes. What you said about Andi was heartening. This might be a second chance for our family."

The two men shook hands and Zemmel contemplated the similarities between himself and Ed Levy. He found the comparison fascinating. I actually helped a guy who's probably in better shape than I am, he speculated ironically as he left his office and headed to his car. Is he actually stronger than I am, Zemmel then wondered cynically, or hasn't he found anyone like Bliss yet. But Levy's right about romance. I'm sick of being a zombie. The real heat's out there with Bliss and I'm not about to let go of it.

Zemmel was satiated with continually sorting and problem solving for others. He wanted the mystery, the irresistible, the purely forbidden. Could evil possibly spin such a tantalizing web, he mused with some awe. How easily it suits our needs. Is that the trap?

If so, I'm hooked, he chuckled to himself with a complete lack of concern. He noticed he was running late and wondered if Bliss would be angry. The prospect was enjoyable. Maybe evil isn't seducing me after all. Perhaps it's the volatility of her emotion. Whatever it is, I need it, he decided emphatically, and entered the Holland Tunnel faster than the speed limit.

CHAPTER 24

Marty glimpsed the moonlight reflected on the wooden floor of Bliss's apartment. He encircled her waist with his arm and desired her once more. Gradually, Bliss opened her eyes and luxuriated in the feel of her lover. "I feel sexy," she said.

"You are sexy; you're killing me."

"I?"

"Yes."

"I'm going to destroy you tonight."

"Completely?"

"Of course," she bit his ear lobe, glad to feel his thigh next to hers.

"You possess the most exquisite breasts," he said and kissed her nipple.

"Make love to them," she answered and pulled him on top of her.

"I want to go down on you," he ventured and she tensed.

"What's wrong?" he asked, stroking her.

"I don't want you to do that."

"Why not? I thought you enjoyed it."

"I do. That's the problem. I don't want to get that vulnerable with you. We can never really be together. We can never be right."

"You judge us very harshly," he cajoled.

"Don't you believe in the concept of right and wrong?" she asked, and pushed his hand away.

"Only as a general guide to keep people from hurting each other."

"To protect us from evil?"

"Possibly."

"Did you ever think our relationship might be evil?" she asked and turned away from him. She felt naked under her mirror.

"Only if you perceive it that way, Bliss."

"How do you perceive it?" she asked with a clear edge in her voice.

"I see us as lovers. We're sexual beings who should enjoy each other."

She turned toward him, "The problem for me is I'm afraid to enjoy you if I think it's wrong."

"Bliss, it's wrong to be dead when you're alive," he said, and tentatively stroked her breasts.

His words melted her doubts. This time she didn't resist and they began a slow embrace.

"Come inside me," she breathed softly and Marty entered her.

"You make me so soft with your hardness," she groaned beneath him.

Marty floated on top of her; captivated by her warmth.

"I told you I would destroy you and I will," she began in a hypnotic chant. You penetrated my softness where I am a woman, where my deepest secret lies. I know you long for it. You want to feel my complete vulnerability. But when you do, I will destroy you by grasping yours. I will know what makes you a man."

Driven insane by her words, he managed to slow himself. Her breasts were completely in his domain and he teased them sorely, "You're right. I want the secret. But I will never steal it from you. Rather. you will give it to me."

"Stop touching me like that."

Once more, he detected her edge. "No," he whispered fiercely in her ear.

"You're taking me where I can't go."

"I'm not taking you anywhere. We're going together. We're recreating ourselves."

He was right; they achieved unity. Yet Bliss feared him. She glanced at the ceiling and was sure her mirror was laughing.

He's using you, it jeered at her. His feelings will never match yours.

He sensed she was dangerously intense. Suddenly he felt like a shrink rather than a lover. She noticed the change in him, and her distrust increased. He's just manipulating you, continued the mirror and Bliss grew enraged, "You've made me yours, but you won't let me possess you. I was sure I would know you through making love, but I don't. Get out!"

Marty automatically gauged the measure of her suffering while he reached for his clothes, and despised himself for it. He wasn't in his study reading textbook cases on misery. Instead, he was part of it, an active participant. He knew how important his next words would be and at the same time he knew they would fall short of her expectation.

"Bliss, I never planned to go this far."

"The universe is cruel."

"You're right. So let's not be cruel to each other."

"I don't have the strength for this. You're married. No matter what happens, someone will be hurt. I thought I could be sophisticated about it, but I can't."

Marty was fully dressed by now and strongly compelled by her honesty. He bent down to tie his shoelaces, fighting off his need for a last embrace, and then he was gone.

Bliss lay on the bed choking. Her source of oxygen was gone and now only suffocation remained. She would not allow herself to cry and preferred to blankly stare at the mirror on the ceiling. She heard him unlock the door and then strained to listen to his receding footsteps.

The activity of the street even at this late hour was a welcome relief from the anxiety of the apartment. Marty relished his freedom from the pull that Bliss exerted on him. She was wrong when she assumed that he left her nothing of himself, because she touched him deeply. Yet he deceived her and allowed her to think it was one sided; it was easier that way.

He wasn't ready for her brand of instability. He was attracted to the chaos, the destruction of barriers, the uninhibited charisma. But they scared him. He wanted to be entertained; he didn't want commitment.

Marty stepped into his car and decided to go straight to the hospital. He would sleep in his office. In the morning he'd have plenty of time to shave, shower, and eat breakfast before sitting down with his first patient. Then he'd call Anne and tell her it was a medical emergency. The excuse is wearing thin, he admitted, but she'll believe me because she wants to.

Hunched over the wheel, Marty began coughing and reached into his pocket for a cough drop. His hand touched the key to the front door of her apartment building. He put the key on the dashboard and stared at it. It exuded an attraction he couldn't ignore. He didn't want to go back to the dead life. Once more he was in the street. This time he was running toward Bliss rather than away from her; his fears submerged by passion.

He let himself into the building easily and climbed the stairs to her apartment. "Let me in," he shouted at Bliss's door when there was no response to his knock.

Bliss refused to answer. How did he get up here, she wondered and then remembered he had the downstairs key.

"Please, let me in," came through the heavy metal door.

"Go away Marty; it's over. I never affected you anyway," Bliss finally called from the kitchen.

"That's where you're wrong," he breathed into the keyhole. "I need to talk with you."

"Marty, don't give me your bullshit. It was all physical with you!"

"Bliss, I'd be on my way to the hospital now if it was all physical."

"How do I know that?"

"I guess you can only know by my telling you. But it's been more than physical for awhile."

"Why did you hide from me?" she screamed hysterically. "Do you enjoy belittling people?"

"I was afraid Bliss. This is very new to me."

"When you left, I went through death you fucking coward," she continued screaming and her hand connected with the first available object. Sugar spewed all over the kitchen floor as she hurled a colonial blue and white bowl at her back door.

"Forgive me."

"I probably would, if you weren't married."

"You knew I was married from the start."

"I hoped it wouldn't matter then, but now I know it does. All you can do is hurt me."

Every word rang true for him, but still he believed in choices. There must be an alternate route to conventions that were strangling him.

"Bliss, right now we're still holding each other. We've touched and I don't want to walk away from you."

"You're making me feel very ugly, Marty. I don't like what I'm doing."

"Beauty isn't sterile. It's dynamic. Please open the door so we can talk."

"No," she said decisively, "I can't face you in here." But his remark about beauty intrigued her. After a pause she continued, "Meet me in Coney Island tomorrow night at eight o'clock underneath the Wonder Wheel."

CHAPTER 25

It smelled of ham the next morning when Andi woke up early. She enjoyed the quiet, but the odor repelled her. Distracted by some birds chirping at the window, Andi envisioned her room at home where birds often sang at dawn. My room must be lonely without me, she thought, and pictured her mother gazing into the emptiness.

There was a tug at Andi's heart. We used to be best friends when I was little, she mused. It seemed as though she and her mother shared one mind and heart. In the car, they both squealed when their favorites came on the radio. There was no greater fun for Andi than dressing up in her mother's shoes, pocketbooks and hats. Best of all, she loved watching her mother in the kitchen. It was warm and loving.

Why did I start hating her so much, Andi wondered. Automatically, her stomach hurt. Mom's so unfair, she thought. She's always forcing me to be religious. There are plenty of Jewish kids who can eat anywhere, go to the movies on Friday night and ride on Shabbat. Only we have to be super Jews.

Then Andi recalled their tremendous fight about Hebrew School. Everyone else quit after Bar/Bat Mitzvah, but I was forced to continue.

Andi's memory jogged back to her first day of Hebrew School. Propped against her pillow, she recalled herself as an eight year old hating to go. She was so sure the teacher would be mean, that Mr. Blatt's kindness astounded her. He was extremely well versed in Torah studies, and was able to carry the class all the way to Bar and Bat Mitzvah.

He was a marker in my childhood, she decided in bed that morning. Strange how I never thought of him as anyone that really mattered. What would he think of me, she wondered sadly, if he knew that I was here?

The classroom grew vivid in her memory and she heard her questions ringing all around her. She was never sure if she believed in G-d. "Bluma," the teacher always called her by her Hebrew name, "you should be a lawyer." Some lawyer, she laughed ruefully. I can't even make a decision about what to eat.

Mr. Blatt said it was O.K. to ask questions, Andi mused. That's what I liked about him. I wonder if he would force me to eat kosher food? Then she smelled the ham and knew she could never eat it.

"Hi Andi, up early I see," said Mary, who was working a double shift. "Ready to wash up and have breakfast?"

"Can't I go myself?"

Mary was candid, "Andi, you're doing very well and I've put that in my report. I even recommended some additional independence for you. But the final decision is with your doctor. So for now, I'm still your shadow."

The two walked to the bathroom in harmony and Andi relaxed back into her reverie. But this time she included the nurse, "Mary..."

"Yes?"

"I've been thinking about food this morning."

"Me too. That ham smells nice, especially for..."

"It's making me sick," interrupted Andi.

"Oh, I'm sorry. I forgot your family doesn't eat that kind of food."

"My mother really hates it. I used to think I'd eat it just to make her mad. But I'd probably choke on the first bite."

"It sounds like an unusual way to hurt someone," remarked Mary.

"We are a weird family in some ways," giggled Andi to herself. Suddenly, everything was hysterical.

On guard against mood swings, Mary used a calming tone, "We're at the lav, Andi. I'll wait right here for you."

There was a merry-go-round spinning in Andi's head. Stop bugging me Ma, she wanted to scream. Even the sink looked accusing when she washed her hands. Cold water ran over her fingers, but she didn't notice because she was too preoccupied with the conversation in her head. Look Ma, I'm not eating anything really unkosher. I'm hardly eating at all.

You could eat plenty, came her mother's voice. I keep telling you I ordered a kosher menu.

I don't want you to order me anything. If I want it, I'll order it myself when I'm good and ready. Now get out of here. Leave me alone.

Andi was so angry, she forgot how to function. "Mary, Mary," she finally called out loud. "I can't turn off the water. The faucet's stuck."

Mary entered quietly and noticed Andi was crying. She turned off the water and deftly steered And back to her cot.

On her cot, Andi crawled into a knot and faced the wall. "Talk to me," coaxed Mary. "Tell me more about you and your Mom. It sounds like a difficult relationship, but I get the feeling you love her a lot."

"I really do love her, but we don't get along lately. Whenever I try to carve out some space for myself, it always steps on her toes. She thinks I hurt her purposely. And the worst part is that whenever I hurt her, I feel worse."

"Sounds like you can't win."

"You're right," whined Andi, "and that really makes me mad. Every time I decide to choose for myself, she acts like I'm destroying her."

Rose Schneider appeared as if from nowhere. "Good morning," she smiled. Andi merely stared at her. The social worker continued, "Your mother's here to visit you."

"What a coincidence," said Andi ironically.

* * * *

Off in a corner, Yolanda and Tina were avidly plotting about "D Day". "That's the code word, Bubba," said Tina. Do you understand about the code? We need to keep all this a secret."

"I'm not an idiot," retorted Yolanda. "But there's something you forgot."

"What?"

"Andi—the star player. I don't think she's gonna go along with this whole mess about Joe you schemed up."

"Why not?"

"You said everything hinged on her gettin' rid of that nurse of hers!"

"So?"

"Look at Andi lyin' all over her bed. And the nurse is holding her hand. Looks like she can't even get Andi to come to breakfast. That's probably why that other roach-head came over."

"Bubba, you're right," whispered Tina, as she stared in the direction of Andi's cot. "What are we gonna do?"

"You mean what are <u>you</u> gonna do," exclaimed Yolanda with emphasis. I ain't the one that brainstormed this disaster. My main objective is to get out of here. I don't mix into other people's business the way you do."

"Listen Bub, this guy Joe has the sexiest voice on the phone, and besides, he really wants to see her. If Plan A doesn't work, we'll just go to Plan B."

"What's that?"

"I'll let you know when I think of it."

"Don't you think we should discuss it with Andi first."

"That's happening quicker than you think. Look who's coming our way."

Andi decided she could face her mother after some orange juice. She headed for the dining area, when she noticed her friends and remembered their plans. Just my luck, she thought, walking at a snail's pace. When I finally know I need Mary, those two want me to ditch her. Why does everyone insist on telling me what to do? Well I know one thing, she thought heatedly, no one's gonna force me to get rid of Mary.

Empowered by her decision, she selected her juice. Maybe that's what everyone means by being mature, Andi suddenly verbalized to herself—when you really understand what you want and have the guts to act on it. This knowledge felt good and gave her the courage to greet Tina and Yolanda. First, the three friends smiled at each other, and then they stared at nothing in particular. The subject of Joe loomed above them and they were uncertain about how to approach it.

"We're all so vulnerable," noted Tina in a brief inward look. "We really are afraid of being hurt."

"Woohee," whistled Yolanda. "I've got the biggest mouth, so I'll take the first risk. Can you ditch your nurse, Andi?"

Surprised that they picked up on her thinking so well, Andi blurted, "I can't get rid of Mary. She's too important to me. I need to know she's there. Even now, I feel safer with her nearby."

"Well Genius," sang Yolanda cheerfully to Tina, "time for Plan B."

Puzzled by the antics, but grateful no one was criticizing her, Andi laughed from nervous exhaustion.

"What's so hilarious?" mumbled Tina.

"I really don't know," laughed Andi even harder. "But I just found out I'm going to see my mom and I'd rather laugh than cry. Besides, everything just seems hysterical today."

"Right," mused Yolanda, "A regular riot."

CHAPTER 26

Sarah attempted to kiss Andi, but her daughter didn't respond. Where's our closeness, Sarah asked herself. Then she remembered her relationship with her own mother. Her mother always wanted a perfect world, and when life fell short, it was a bitter disappointment.

There was never any growing space, Sarah thought to herself. It was always, 'marry and settle down.' Security was her mother's banner, her call to arms, 'Sarah, make sure you have what I never had.' I always hated her for that, Sarah thought. Is that the way Andi sees me?

"Look at me, Ma," came Andi's insistent voice. "I'm not a baby anymore."

"Andi, I know that. I'm thinking...I'm remembering myself with my mother and how she never seemed to see me. She could only envision a series of dashed hopes that she longed to fulfill through me."

"Then we share a similar problem."

"The problem is being forced to smile in other people's pictures," said Sarah.

"Well I want to smile in my own picture Ma—not the one you dreamed up for me. I'm sorry you had it rough with Grandma. But you only support me when my ideas go along with yours. And when my ideas don't go along with yours, you don't want to know about them."

"Are you talking about Joe?"

"Not necessarily. You're the one that made me think a guy was everything. You just thought I chose the wrong guy because he wasn't Jewish."

"Andi, I thought Joe's so important to you."

"He is Ma, but right now I'm more concerned about us—our whole family—the way we relate with each other. Or the way we don't relate with each other. I went through a barrier the night I tried to kill myself. Yes, I did a stupid thing. I know that. But I found a place in myself I never knew existed. There's a whole world inside me that was always closed."

"Isn't Joe part of that world for you? Are you angry at me because I couldn't accept him?"

Andi verged on screaming. She wanted to talk about her feelings, but her mother didn't know how. She wanted to say it wasn't about Joe. What mattered was how she felt about herself. Instead she blurted, "You'll never understand my inner world."

Andi's breathing quickened and there was a rush in her head. Oh G-d, please don't let me stress out; especially in front of her.

"Andi, Andi, what's the matter? You look strained."

"It's O.K. Ma. I just have to regulate my breathing. If I can't, I'll call Mary."

"Let's try and work it out together, Andi. I hate turning to strangers."

"She's not a stranger; she's my nurse. We talk a lot. I tell her things I could never tell you. She doesn't spend most of the conversation judging me."

"If that was meant to hurt me, it did. Please, Andi, let's stop bickering," pleaded Sarah.

"Start hearing what I say then, not what you think I should be saying."

"That's what I want to do," began Sarah with a genuine attempt at calmness. "No matter what, I love you. I don't like this gulf between us or anything that's happened lately."

"Ma, why are you avoiding everything?" asked Andi testily.

"It was all so awful. I wish none of it happened."

"Mom," cried Andi in rising desperation, "this is my life and I need to talk about it."

"What about the night we brought you here?" asked Sarah despite a sinking feeling. "Would you like to talk about that?"

"Yes, that night was a horror show for me."

"You were very frightened that night. Dad and I couldn't bear to leave you."

"But you did."

"We had no choice," said Sarah feeling guilty.

"There are always choices," accused Andi.

Sarah saw the gathering clouds in her daughter's eyes. She wished she'd let Andi call Mary earlier. Now she wanted to call the nurse herself, but didn't dare. She sensed any move away from the conversation might look like betrayal to her daughter who was stiff with anger.

"It was like the world stopped—much worse than death," intoned Andi in a dreadfully low voice. "When they bandaged my wrists, I knew I would live. There would be no escape from all the unhappiness. My mind actually blanked when you and Dad left. I was so terrified."

Sarah cried inwardly as her daughter spoke. Andi's words pierced into her own sense of helpless fear. She was numb when they left Andi at the hospital. It was like giving birth and leaving the baby. She attempted to lie to herself when they bandaged Andi's wrists. It was an accident; not a suicide attempt. Her hand just slipped on the knife. But when she looked at her daughter's wan face and dead eyes that night, she couldn't keep fooling herself.

"Ma," Andi's voice brought Sarah to the present, "why are you drifting? I want you to understand that night from my perspective."

"Andi," said Sarah, "that night was very painful—I thought I could talk about it, but I can't."

"Right, you want to ignore it, just like you always ignore everything I think and feel."

"Andi, I'm trying to see things your way, but you're making me hyper. Can't you calm down?

"Actually, no—you're driving me crazy. You say you're here to help me, but every time I say something, you don't want to hear it."

"Well what is it you want to say?"

"There's an awful loneliness inside me that makes me want to strike out. I keep running away from it. But I can never run fast enough. It's always right behind me."

"Andi, where does all this loneliness come from? You always had friends. Dad and I have always given you everything you wanted within reason. Why are you doing this to yourself? Why are you doing it to me?

Sarah's questions sounded shallow to Andi's ringing ears. Simultaneously, her mother's face appeared distant and pasty. It was no longer a face; it was just a blob. Andi was alone and abandoned. She could no longer tolerate Sarah's poverty of spirit. She was sick of her mother's pathetically inane questions and hope against hope that it would all pass.

In the pause that endured between them, Sarah wondered why Andi was so still, when suddenly Andi's fist zoomed into her line of vision cracking the air like a whip. "All you care about is yourself," Andi hissed. You make me want to kill you."

Mary heard Sarah's scream and noticed Andi's hand was raised above her head. Oh G-d, Andi's going to kill her mother, she thought, and dashed toward them just as Andi's fist struck Sarah's nose.

Mary registered the dull rage in Andi's eyes in contrast to the hurt disbelief in her mother's, as the nurse neatly pinned Andi to the floor.

"You just don't get it," yelled Andi at what still looked like a blob instead of a face. "Can't you ever see me? Can't you see I hate you?"

"Yes Andi," screamed Sarah, "I see you hate me. You hate me the same way I hated my mother. But I kept it all in."

"Well I can't keep it in, Ma. There are terrible feelings inside me that I can't escape."

"But I never punched my mother. I wouldn't dream of it," wept Sarah through the blood trickling into her mouth.

"Ma, I tried to talk to you but you wouldn't listen. Why did you come here anyway? Just to make me crazier than I already am?"

"I came because I love you. I wanted us to talk. But you're right," Sarah admitted. "You keep saying things I'm not ready to hear."

"Mm," said Andi.

The blob looked red and swollen, like an oozing overripe tomato. But words came out of it that finally sounded right for Andi, so she listened to them through Mary's arms.

"I knew you were unhappy, but I didn't want to admit it. I wanted you to be the way I pictured you, and I shut out everything else."

It's not tomato juice, it's blood, realized Andi. My God, she's really hurt...and it's my fault. "I'm sorry Ma. I just got so mad."

"Andi," said her mother, taking the ice offered by the medic, "Don't worry about being sorry."

"I wish I didn't hit you," whispered Andi.

"You tried words, lots of them, but they didn't work. I was really afraid to listen."

"Look at you, Ma. You're bleeding and it's all because of me. I think I broke your nose. I'm scared. It's my fault! I'm ugly! I'm disgusting," cried Andi.

"Let go of her. She's turning blue," yelled Sarah, pushing away Mary's arm.

"I can't breathe," gasped Andi.

"Yes you can," Mary said, "just relax."

"How can I? Look at what I did to my mother."

"Don't blame yourself Andi," begged Sarah. "You wanted to be close, but I pushed you away. I was too afraid."

"What frightened you, Mrs. Levy," asked Mary.

"All that loneliness...and unhappiness. Andi tearing at both of us. I feel it too, but talking's really hard for me."

"I don't want to tear at you, Ma. It's the wall between us that I want to destroy," wept Andi.

"I know. I've been up against that wall myself. Many times. But confrontation is too painful for me and I just run away. I guess you're confronting for both of us. Andi, are you listening to me?

"Yeah, Ma."

Sarah reached for Andi's shoulder, "I just don't want you to be alone. This is my struggle too. You're my daughter and we'll fight this together."

For the first time in a long time, her words rang true for both of them.

CHAPTER 27

Marty woke up with a headache and couldn't remember where he was. He glanced at the ceiling and then the wall. His books stared back at him. "Oh, it's the office," he groaned out loud and scenes from the night before leaped at him.

But his office was a source of comfort and soon Marty's headache eased. He started reading book titles, which usually soothed him. After a few moments, his eyes strayed to his desk where he spotted a picture by Andi Levy.

The deep earth tone colors of the drawing captivated him. He spotted images of her disabling anxiety, but he also discerned her quest for beauty, and the inhibition of her emotions bubbling so close to the surface. The abandon in Andi's drawing linked Marty to his own eroticism. He knew there was danger, but there was also pleasure and that intrigued him.

He wanted to let go with Bliss—grab her breasts and bury himself in them. He wanted to smell them, and kiss them all over. But mostly, he wanted her to kiss him. I am not so hard, he wanted to whisper to her. I am also soft. I am also vulnerable. And I am ashamed. Are you sure you want to see me Bliss, he almost murmured out loud.

*   *   *   *

"Good morning."

Looking up from her paper work, Madi almost dropped it on the floor. Who are these men with beards, black hats and long strings hanging from their shirts, she wondered.

"Uh, hello, are you looking for someone? Visiting hours haven't started yet," Madi finally informed them, unsure of how they got this far.

"We know; we have permission," the older man said, extending a pass to her, but careful not to touch.

From where? Mars? Madi almost giggled out loud. "How can I help you?" she finally managed with a straight face.

"We're on a special mission," replied the younger one.

Maybe they are from Mars after all, she mused, almost laughing again. Unsure if they understood her despite their perfect English, she raised her voice and spoke very slowly, "Why are you here?"

"Ah, I'm glad you asked," answered the older with a mild accent Madi couldn't quite place. "We're looking for Jewish people."

Immediately on guard, Madi stared harder. They no longer appeared quite so charming. The younger man recognized the chill and quickly interceded. "We're here on a journey of good deeds, a mitzvah campaign. We've come to share with Jewish patients."

"So you like Jews."

"Of course, we <u>are</u> Jews," he said heartily, and both men smiled.

"Well, everything about our patients is confidential," replied Madi rather curtly, "including their religion."

"Is there a doctor we could speak with?" asked the younger man.

"Hmm, there's Dr. Zemmel. He's Jewish," Madi added helpfully. "But I certainly couldn't disturb him. Would you care to wait?"

*   *   *   *

"I hit my Mom this morning," said Andi in her therapy session.

Zemmel waited for more, but Andi thought she heard condemnation in his silence.

"You think I should be punished. I didn't hit her lightly either. I punched her in the face. Her nose might be broken. Stop staring at me. Say something!"

156

"Andi, I know this is very difficult for you, but the anger you felt towards your mother today may have something to do with other feelings."

"Like from what happened just before I came here?"

"Mmm."

"I was very alone, but I was hoping that Joe and I would soon be back together. And then my friend called. She told me Joe went to the movies with someone else. All I could think about was that he lied to me. Maybe he never even liked me. Maybe he used me. But worst of all, I knew he was gone and there was no one else for me. Whenever I felt bad before, I thought of him and felt better. He was the reason for my life. He was the only one that cared. My mother never cared about me. She only cared about herself."

"You and your mother don't share that warmth you felt with Joe."

"No, lately there's a lot of ice."

"Andi, when you hit your mother, I think you were desperately trying to crack that ice."

"Yeah, but I didn't crack ice. I cracked her nose, and I feel really bad about that. I don't think she'll ever forgive me. I was awful. All I wanted to do was smash and smash."

"There's a lot of anger in your relationship."

"But she doesn't want to face it. She wants everything to go back to when I was little and we were best friends."

"Aren't you looking for some of those good feelings too?"

"Yes, but not if it means never growing up."

"But weren't you also afraid of growing up when you thought it meant growing up without Joe?"

"I guess you could say that."

"So you and your mother may share similar fears."

"Maybe. Before I hit her, she said she had problems about pleasing her own mother."

"It seems that you and your mother may both be familiar with angry and scared feelings. Your conflict is that you're starting to confront them while she's still avoiding them."

"That's exactly right. That's what I told her before I punched her."

"Our task now is to put those hostile feelings into words."

"I was putting them into words. She just refused to listen."

"You took a first step. It was risky and difficult, but it was a start. I think we need to talk more about your ambivalence concerning growing up. It's like you do and you don't. You want to but you're scared."

"That's my problem. I think I grab onto other people, to grow up through them. Tina's the latest."

"Tina?"

"Oh, yeah, she's..."

"Where are you Andi? Why did you stop cold?"

"I don't know."

"Something about Tina disturbed you."

"She's much more grown up than I am."

"How does that strike you?"

Andi resented the question, but she answered him. "I feel immature next to her."

"Say more," he pressed.

"You're always in my head," she exploded. "You never let me keep anything from you. I don't know anything about you. It's not fair."

Amazed to hear the echo of Bliss in her complaint, Marty noted their time was up. "I'm afraid we're through for today," he said, and attempted some humor. "I guess you're saved by the bell."

"You're only saying that cause I asked about you," she retorted, refusing to laugh.

"If you think you need to know something about me in order to heal yourself, you can ask me tomorrow."

Surprised by his equanimity, Andrea walked out in silence. She never quite understood how he did it, but once more she felt cheated. Why did he always get to see more than she did?

"Hi Andi," said Mary, gauging her young patient's mood.

"I think he's mad at me."

"Zemmel?"

"Yeah. I asked about him and he said my time was up."

"It was."

"How come I never get to ask any questions?"

"That's the way it usually is with shrinks," Mary said casually.

"We ended up talking about Tina."

"Really."

Andi paused and Mary was aware of a thick undercurrent.

"She's creative," Andi finally continued. "I like the way she thinks. The problem is I'm not sure she respects what I think, and the worst part is I don't even know what I think."

"You may be more complex."

"Me?" asked Andi incredulously, "I'm simple compared to her."

"Don't short change yourself Andi. Tina's views may be more sophisticated than yours, but that comes with growing up."

"There's Tina now," said Andi, both relieved and disturbed at the sight of her friend. I promised to meet her."

Mary stepped back to allow the illusion of privacy. She was sure the girls were scheming, but she decided to turn a deaf ear. In her opinion, Andi was a case of exaggerated growing pains. Doctors were smart, but often lacked common sense. Andi needed friends. After all, how could anyone mature in a test tube, Mary reasoned.

* * * *

Marty completed his notes on the last patient and decided to talk to Madi about Danny's progress in the treatment program.

He immediately noticed the two Hassidim seated near her station and was stunned at the resemblance between the younger man and the Hasid, Chaim Katz, who visited Bliss's apartment the week before. His paranoia was instantaneous. Is this guy tracking me? Worse yet, is this a bizarre form of punishment? Marty turned quickly in the hope that he wasn't seen, but escape was impossible.

"Dr. Zemmel," called Madi, "What great timing. These gentlemen are looking for Jewish patients. I thought you might help, since you are, uh, Jewish."

Her words stirred a war in Marty's head. Irrational fears cut off his windpipe, and he barely managed to squeak out an invitation into his office from the midst of a coughing spasm. Zemmel felt strangely at the mercy of the two men as they followed him through the corridor into his office. Finally behind his desk with a cough drop in his mouth, he fought back an urge to share his fears with the men before him and grew practical, "So, what can I do for you?"

Answering his question with another, the older man asked, "So, is this where you help people who have problems adjusting?"

"In a manner of speaking," Marty was surprised but pleased by their interest.

"Assuming you so called cure them, what then?"

"That's a good point. We like to work with the whole family, but often the patient is thrown back into the same disastrous circumstances that first exacerbated the problem. Of course, we do continue to treat people as outpatients. By the way, are you rabbis?"

"I am," said the elder man, extending his hand. "Chaim is studying."

Marty was immediately struck by the coincidence of the names, but only said, "I suppose you see all this in a different light."

"To a degree. We realize there are medical problems, but we know that a spiritual dessert can be a painful experience. As a matter of fact, we are here on an outreach program to lend support to those who most need it," said the rabbi.

Marty was impressed with them and immediately thought about Andi Levy. "I have a young patient, Andi Levy, who is possibly interested in following the traditional dietary laws. Maybe you would like to start with her, and in the meantime I may think of some others. Visiting hours aren't till after lunch, but I'll arrange for you to see her shortly," added Marty with growing enthusiasm.

"And you, Doctor, if I might be presumptuous. What about you?" asked the younger man rather suddenly.

The urge to speak more openly about his Jewishness came upon Marty once more, but he remained aloof, "It's only fair to tell you I follow the precepts of reform Judaism."

"You make it sound like another religion. Aren't we all Jews?" pressed Chaim.

"Of course we are, but I don't see the value of many rituals that I assume you espouse."

"Do you deny the value of your soul?"

"It's a little early for religious debates," said Marty, rising to indicate the interview was over. "If you like, I'll set things up with the Levy girl and perhaps there are some other possibilities. I'll see what I can do."

Privately he wondered at the timing of the visit of the rabbi and his young student. Marty never doubted there was a soul; he just wasn't about to discuss it with someone who never stopped looking in a rule book. Yet still, continued Marty in a debate with himself, the guy was perceptive. Why did they show up at just that moment?

*   *   *   *

Mary blinked when she saw the two men dressed in black walk toward her. They're totally strange, she thought, even for this place.

"Pardon me, Miss, we're looking for Andi Levy," said Chaim.

"She's...she's right here. But who are you?"

"We're on a campaign of Good Deeds. Here is our card and a letter of permission from Dr. Zemmel. He recommended that we speak with Andi."

Andi immediately identified the men before her as members of the Hasidic Community. Such people frequently visited her Hebrew School. Under ordinary circumstances she would have conversed with them, but she didn't believe their story of being recommended by Dr. Zemmel. Rather, she was positive they were on a mission for her mother.

"Dr. Zemmel isn't religious," she said. "Why would he send you? Don't think you can fool me; I know my mother is behind this. Why can't she just butt the hell out of my life."

"Can't we just talk?" asked Chaim, very aware that she was a mental patient.

"I have nothing to say."

"What about listening?" asked the elder rabbi calmly.

"I've heard enough of your mumbo jumbo from my Mom. And if you must know," yelled Andi, going completely out of control, "I might even eat kosher food here in the hospital, but not because my mother wants me to. I can't believe she sent you here to bug me!"

"Gentlemen," interrupted Mary, "at this point it doesn't matter who sent you, I'm afraid you'll have to leave. Dr. Zemmel is emphatically against over stimulation."

"Can we at least leave some material?" asked Chaim as he handed some pamphlets to Andi, who promptly threw them on the floor.

* * * *

Andi watched them go, still very much distraught, "Why is she always hassling me? I want to start making decisions on my own. But if she doesn't know every thought in my head, she's on my back."

"Slow down Andi," said Mary firmly. "You don't know your mother sent them..."

"True," conceded Andi. "But why would Dr. Zemmel..."

"They did have a letter."

"They could have forged it."

"Oh Andi, you're really jumping to conclusions now. Don't you trust anyone?"

"Why should I?"

"Has Dr. Zemmel ever lied to you?" asked Mary.

"No," she answered thoughtfully, "but why would Dr. Zemmel send those two?"

"You can ask him yourself," replied Mary with some relief, "He's right here."

"Dr. Zemmel, did you know those two men with beards?" asked Andi excitedly.

"Mmhum."

"Did my mother send them?"

"Why no," he answered, clearly baffled.

"Oh, right! You would never admit it anyway."

"I thought we were past all that."

"Well, what were they doing in the hospital if she didn't send them?"

"You know something Andi," said Zemmel, glad to have someone share his bewilderment, "I also asked myself why they were here."

Dr. Zemmel was obviously as puzzled as Andi, and for the first time she was able to see him as an ordinary person. He was no longer the head doctor with all the answers. In that moment he could be anyone, even her own father. The thought relaxed her, and she decided she liked Dr. Zemmel better when he didn't seem to know everything.

Then Andi spotted the literature on the floor exactly where she had thrown it. Since her mother didn't send those men, Andi reasoned, maybe the pamphlets were worth reading. They might even contain information about keeping kosher that would appeal to her.

Just as Andi reached for the pamphlets, Tina appeared. All thoughts about food and the Hassidim left her. What's so different about her, Andi wondered. Why do I like to be with her so much?

CHAPTER 28

Andi liked Tina's exotic aura. She wanted to be near Tina and smell the blend of perfume and incense she exuded. Ever since Andi tried on Tina's clothes, she had a desire to return to Tina's room. It was a channel into the unknown for Andi.

At first Andi believed Tina was like so many of her friends, but now she accepted that Tina was very different from anyone she knew. Tina invited closeness, a sense of intimacy. She went beyond the ordinary and stirred excitement.

Andi enjoyed the adventurous feelings Tina inspired. Beneath her consciousness, she even hoped that her intense longing for Joe might be satisfied by Tina.

Perhaps it was the strength of this longing that blinded Andi to the subtleties of Tina's convoluted inner makeup. Tina wanted friends more than anything, but she was never sure if she wanted to keep them. To woo friends, she became a master of impressions and transformed herself into any number of pleasing shapes. She made her psyche very compatible to others, but it was always temporary. Games and challenges were easier for Tina to handle than the depth of real friendship. When Tina was finally called upon to give of herself, she inevitably ran away.

Mary was also unaware of the full extent of Tina's problems and the impact they might have on Andi. On the contrary, she noticed Andi was happier with Tina and believed the relationship might be therapeutic if properly controlled. Therefore, when Andi asked if she could visit Tina, Mary agreed. She even encouraged her patient by trailing behind at a respectable distance. Mary always believed it was important to give Andi some freedom.

"Hi," said Andi to Tina. "I...want to talk to you."

"Come in," said Tina, happy to see that Andi's nurse remained outside. "What do you want to talk about?"

"Uh, I don't really know," stammered Andi, who immediately hated herself for being tongue tied.

"Hmm, give it a moment." Playing shrink was one of Tina's favorite roles and it made Andi feel more secure.

"I like your room. It's different."

"How?"

"It seems like anything could happen here. Nothing's forbidden."

"Andi, come on my bed and feel this fuzzy bear," invited Tina with a smile. "Isn't he terrific?...Take off your shoes."

Andi relaxed while they cuddled up to the bear, "Guess what?" she said, "I'm really not sure I want to see Joe anymore."

"What about busting him?"

"It was a dumb idea."

"Why?" Tina was genuinely curious. She liked the sound of his voice on the phone just as she liked the feel of Andi next to her.

"I'm sick of living in the past...What kind of perfume do you have on?" Andi pointedly changed the subject.

"Tabu, want some?"

"Sure."

Tina applied it directly to Andi's cheeks and throat.

"Ummm, that smells so nice," said Andi, captivated by her friend's gentleness.

"My mom always likes me to put perfume on her. So what about Joe? Since when is he just the past?"

"I've been thinking about the way he treated me. I gave him everything, or was about to, and he threw me away."

"Does that mean you're still a virgin? asked Tina with a candor that scared and engrossed Andi at once. By now their toes were nuzzled against each other.

"Yeah, I am," admitted Andi after a pause. "I loved him so much and wanted to be with him all the time. Finally, I decided to get birth control. Everything seemed perfect. But at the last minute, he backed down and we semi broke up to think things over. At least I thought it was semi. Apparently he had other ideas."

But as she spoke, Joe grew distant and Tina's physical proximity brought Andi back to the present. She realized she was anxious to find out about Tina. "What about you? Are you a virgin?"

"No, but not by a man."

"Not by a man," Andi unconsciously repeated Tina's perplexing words to herself. "How then?"

"There are a couple of possibilities."

Andi's foot froze.

"Why are you so shocked?" continued Tina, her confidence growing with Andi's confusion. "It could have been a dildo or my own finger or..."

"Or what," asked Andi, impatient and totally clueless as to why Tina stopped so abruptly.

"Some other girl's finger."

"Another girl's...finger?"

"Yeah. Are you turned off?" asked Tina in a voice she hoped was detached.

"I've never talked about these things before," confided Andi, "but I think I like it."

"Do you like me?" asked Tina pointedly.

"How?"

"My body...would you like us to touch?"

Andi's hips formed a circular pattern on the bed and her breathing became measured. "Yes, Tina," she answered softly. I want to do something different and exciting."

"Why don't you touch my breasts," asked Tina. "I like the way that feels." Andi stroked Tina's breasts and appreciated their softness. She enjoyed the intimacy and began to experience an irresistible feeling of power. But when Tina touched Andi's breasts, Andi experienced an explosion. Suddenly she discovered a voice that was uniquely hers. "I love you Tina," she said passionately and kissed her.

Very characteristically, Tina ignored Andi's confession. Instead, she introduced another dimension to the relationship. "Try some perfume on your twat," said Tina, moving to undress Andi. Tina's gesture was provocative and Andi enjoyed the feeling of nakedness. It made her forget her disappointment that Tina disregarded her words.

"Who will smell me?" she asked coyly.

"I will," answered Tina, quickly undressing herself.

Tina's fingers moved to Andi's vagina. She was very gentle and her voice was hypnotic. "You're wet and beautiful," Tina whispered, and then she kissed her.

Andi floated beneath Tina's softness and entrusted herself to Tina's caress. "You're making me feel grown up and womanly," she breathed.

From somewhere Tina flicked on a tape. The music was slow and dreamy, and Andi felt more relaxed than she could ever remember...

*　　*　　*　　*

The hand on Andi's shoulder woke her with a start. "Andi, it's late," whispered Tina urgently. "It's lucky your nurse dozed off. I think she has a problem with alcohol."

"How do you know these things?" asked Andi incredulously. It seemed impossible. Mary was her favorite role model. How many illusions could Tina shatter?

"I work in the nurses' station, remember?" answered Tina curtly. "But don't waste time talking about her. Hurry up and put your clothes on or we'll both be in trouble."

"I don't want to," said Andi, still covered with star dust from their earlier encounter. "Hug me."

"My you are aggressive," answered Tina in a sharply unfamiliar voice.

"Don't you like me?" trembled Andi.

"We were just playing."

"But it felt good. I don't want it to end. Let's kiss," insisted Andi despite a new creeping fear of rejection. She remembered the power and the freedom she and Tina experienced, and she wanted it to continue. She especially liked the equality she believed she shared with Tina at that moment. When she and Joe were together, she always waited for him to start first. With Tina, conventions were demolished and there was a limitless quality to the interplay. Hers were no longer the only breasts and anything could happen. But now, when she tried to embrace Tina, all she found was coldness.

"Stop it Andi, I told you I was just playing."

"You mean you lied about losing your virginity and not being sure how?"

"Everything."

"But I believed you."

"Tough."

"Everything I said and did was true," whimpered Andi more to herself than to Tina.

"Hmm," was all Tina offered.

Time stopped for Andi. She knew she should get up, put on her clothes and leave the room as quickly as possible. But events were converging, and she was back in the phone booth on the day when Joe refused to speak with her. Worse still, she was home waiting for a phone that never rang. The empty sharpness of betrayal shocked and numbed her body as doors opened only to be unceremoniously slammed in her face.

"Here," tried Tina once more, "put on your clothes. Mary will probably show up in a minute. Let's not get caught."

Andi blindly followed Tina's logic and began to dress. As she put on her bra and underpants, she understood that Tina was a liar. By her own admission, she lied. The only question that remained for Andi was why.

"You weren't just playing before Tina," accused Andi. "Why are you like this now?"

Tina, however, remained undaunted, "I just am. I hate being the same all the time."

"Is that your excuse for treating me like dirt?" exploded Andi, as she forced her feet to move from the room.

She knew then that Tina was irrational and would never give in to logic contrary to her own. In fact, realized Andi with sudden insight, there really is no Tina. There's only a facade that I fell for, she thought. When Tina spoke and touched me so softly, I believed it was real, but it wasn't.

Once more, as with Joe and her family, Andi was left empty handed. Bitterness and despair caught in her throat, while an awful loneliness beat in her breast. Just when she thought she might be together with someone, Andi found herself alone. She left the room and her frustration burned hotly. It wasn't fair.

The old destructive feelings returned. She didn't know where she was or where she was going. All that mattered to Andi was the terrible isolation that drove her insane.

"What are you doing standing in a corner?" asked Madi, who had just returned from an illegal smoke.

"Uh, I..." completely disoriented, Andi wasn't sure. She stopped talking and stared in front of her.

"Would you like some water?" asked Madi trying to make contact, but Andi merely shook her head. "I'll walk you back to your cot then," said Madi. Andi offered no resistance as Madi took her arm and gently guided her in the direction of her room. Madi privately wondered why Andi's behavior was so erratic. More to the point, she wondered where Mary was.

CHAPTER 29

Andi slept fitfully that night, and in the morning her stomach was molten lead. She didn't want to open her eyes or move a muscle. Death thoughts gradually filtered into her consciousness. It was comforting to visualize nonexistence. Since she was unable to control her relations with others, she would hurt herself and hurt them too. She thought she could connect up with Tina in a good way, but that didn't work, so let it be bad. Let it hurt. The more hurt the better for herself and everyone else.

She hated the rejection. It was a mask of ether over her head, suffocating her. Her neck strained towards the wall. The feelings of negative power were returning. She could do anything. She would push her head right through that wall. She would punch a hole through that wall with her strength. Her death would be much more important than her life.

Just then, she envisioned Dr. Zemmel. He was standing right there, right by the wall, looming over her life as well as her death. He didn't say anything, but she understood the look in his eyes. What are you doing, he seemed to ask. Why are you so willing to throw all our hard work away? Don't our talks mean anything to you? Yes, they do, she thought to herself. They mean a lot to me. Am I really disappointing you?

I think you're disappointing yourself. Why do you give up so easily, when you are so young and beautiful and first beginning to see it?

The urge to bang lessened. I don't actually need to destroy myself because of other people, she thought and pictured Zemmel again. What will he think of me, she wondered. How will I ever tell him about Tina? Yet despite her doubts, Andi wanted to share her experience with Zemmel. He's got to understand, if I ever get up the nerve to tell him.

*   *   *   *

Andi sat in Zemmel's office, afraid to open her mouth and let words come out that were too dangerous to speak. Her stomach churned with the effort of both speaking and not speaking, and she couldn't bear to look at him.

Fear made it difficult for Andi to walk into this session. Her legs felt stiff. She couldn't look at anything directly; not even the stranger who guided her into her seat. Where was Mary? She vaguely realized her nurse was missing, but lacked the energy to ask.

"What are you thinking, Andi?" asked Dr. Zemmel very quietly. His words sounded as though they came from a great distance, but they managed to penetrate the fog, and Andi wondered if she could think at all. She really longed to answer the question, but found it impossible. Even the simplest words brought up complexities too difficult for her to approach. Yet, finally words did come.

"I don't know," she heard her tiny voice speak.

The words brought a release of tension. "Is it O.K. not to know?" continued Andi.

"It's a start," commented Zemmel.

His intuition told him that this could be a direct link into the breakdown that brought her under his care. He hoped to enable Andi to delve into the pain that held her inner voice hostage. So when Andi offered nothing further, Zemmel probed, "Sounds like you're afraid to think."

"I'm thinking about my humiliation," said Andi, and immediately stopped talking.

Zemmel patiently waited for more.

"I'm burning with shame," continued Andi in a new voice. "I'm no good. I'm worse than no good. I'm disgusting," she sobbed. "I went to Tina's room so we could talk. I wanted to tell her I wasn't so sure about Joe anymore, but I also just wanted to be in her room. It has a pretty smell and so does she."

"Describe the smell."

"Kind of like incense from the Orient. She said it was a perfume called Tabu. First she put some on my face and her fingers were very gentle."

"What did you talk about?"

"She asked me if I was a virgin and told me she wasn't."

"So she has done what you have not."

"Yes, but I was surprised at how she lost her...virginity."

"Why?"

"She said it wasn't from a man. Then she wanted to touch my vagina and I let her. I knew it was wrong, but it was very exciting, especially when she kissed me there. Then I touched her breasts...They were soft and smooth."

"And?"

"I told her I loved her."

Andi paused and then continued, "We stretched out naked on her bed and fell asleep. I don't know where Mary was. Nobody bothered us. Tina says Mary drinks. Is that true?"

Zemmel said nothing.

"Anyway, when I woke up, I had an ache for Tina. I wanted to hug and kiss her. But...but..."

"Why is it hard for you to talk now?"

"For Tina it was different. She told me it was all a lie. Everything got ugly and she tried to make me think that I meant nothing to her."

"I guess you were confused."

"I was more than confused. I was desperate."

"Hmm."

I wanted her to be beautiful and kiss me, but she wouldn't." To her it was all some kind of sick joke," laughed Andi bitterly.

"So you felt betrayed. Let's talk about it."

"Talking hurts."

"So does not talking."

"It's too complicated."

"Why?"

"Because it wasn't just one betrayal. It was like a whole series. When she refused to kiss me, it made me think of how Joe also didn't want me. And then I heard myself begging a girl for a kiss and I got sick. How could this be me?" She paused and looked directly at Zemmel for the first time. "Dr. Zemmel, am I a lesbian?"

"You just got through telling me that this was complicated; now you want to put a label on it and be done with it," said Zemmel to give her the balance she needed to continue. "Sexuality is often a mystery."

"I wanted that kiss so much," said Andi.

"It was important to you."

"I saw something beautiful in her and I wanted to make love."

"You wanted to make love to what you *thought* you saw in her. I'm not so sure that means you wanted to make love to her."

"I just told you I wanted to kiss Tina," Andi almost screamed in frustration. "Doesn't that mean anything to you?"

"What does it mean to you?"

"It means I'm a lesbian," answered Andi flatly.

"You're back to putting a label on your sexuality," counseled Zemmel. "I think it's more important to explore it. Tina is very seductive. She said and did things that were new and highly stimulating."

"That's right. Like I said, I'm no good. I responded to her."

"Andi, don't be so hard on yourself. This isn't a court of law. I think Tina served as a catalyst into your deeper feelings, and you mistook those feelings as being for her."

"You're trying to make it sound like I never cared about her."

"You barely know Tina," offered Zemmel matter of factly, "but you are very fascinated by her, and I think that stems from your interest in yourself."

"But I wanted to kiss Tina," insisted Andi vehemently; not myself."

"You sound angry."

"I am...at you."

"I don't think so. I think you're condemning yourself for having feelings."

"For Tina?"

"For yourself."

"You make it sound like I wanted to kiss myself."

"I think you do."

"You mean all that..."

"Passion," offered Zemmel.

"All that passion I felt for Tina was really for myself?"

"Yes and no. The beauty you see in her may really be your ideal of an exotic and independent woman who could go beyond convention. Perhaps Tina is a mirror for you—an affirmation of yourself.

"So when I thought I wanted to make love to Tina, I kind of wanted to make love to myself," said Andi tentatively. "But I still wanted to kiss a woman. What does that mean?"

"Your intense desire to kiss her may be an expression of your sexuality rather than a statement of sexual preference. In essence, your experience with Tina enabled you to start embracing your own beauty, your own sense of being a woman."

"I like that," said Andi simply and quietly. "It's hard for me to see myself as beautiful or sexual."

"Feeling good about your sexuality is a vital step toward being happy," said Zemmel warmly.

"I think I feel more like a dishrag," laughed Andi weakly.

"When your feelings are in a deep freeze, the thaw can sting and wear you out. But my guess is that it's a good, worthwhile kind of being tired."

"You're right, Dr. Zemmel. I am feeling good and very relaxed. Just before when you talked about my being a woman, it made me think about Joe, but I don't want to talk about him right now.

Zemmel sensed they were about to enter a deeper level of her therapy and so he quietly waited for her to continue.

"I want to tell you what happened after Madi found me in a corner and brought me back to my cot...I almost started banging my head against the wall and hurting myself again."

"But you didn't. You resisted having a panic attack," he said very quietly.

"I pictured you asking me why I was so willing to throw all our hard work away." Andi really wanted him to speak just then, although she was sure he wouldn't. Yet she sensed caring through his reserve, and that gave her fortitude to go ahead.

"I was so close to banging my head, scratching my face, biting my wrists, anything to let the pain inside of me out. But I didn't want to lose my control."

"You chose sanity over madness," he commented.

"Yeah, before therapy I never saw choices and I felt too weak to make decisions. Now I'm still weak, but our talking brings out alternatives."

"Our dialogue is expanding your consciousness."

"Yes," Andi whispered, ashamed for him to see how dependent she was on this dialogue.

He saw her fear and attempted to assuage it. "Andi, it was very healthy for you to visualize me when you wanted to hurt yourself."

"It was?"

"Together we're working to build new perceptions of yourself, so I'm part of what's starting to feel good and strong. Therefore, when you felt like you were slipping, you searched until you found something to hold onto. It just looked like me, but it was really your own strength."

"I like to think of you so I don't feel so alone," she confided.

"I guess it's lonely to view yourself from a new perspective. But remember, enduring loneliness is an essential part of growing up."

"I hate it. By the way, where's Mary? I really miss her."

"I'm sorry Andi, but Mary is on a leave of absence. Weren't you introduced to your new nurse?"

"I guess so, but I just saw a meaningless face."

"You're going to like Sherrine. Kid's love her."

"I hate leaving this office."

"Andi, you don't have to give in to those negative feelings. They needn't eclipse all the good things we've said here today."

Without another word, Andi stood and left. She knew he was right, but that didn't make it much easier. If only she could talk to Mary about all this, but now even Mary was gone.

Zemmel watched his patient leave and believed she was gaining in strength. Unfortunately, he wasn't so certain about himself. He glanced at the clock and realized he was running late. How long would Bliss wait, he wondered.

CHAPTER 30

Bliss stood beneath the Wonder Wheel. The weather was raw and the sky was smudged with soot. Everything was empty on the boardwalk. She actually enjoyed the wasteland desolation accented by the waves crashing against the shoreline. It suited her mood of quiet desperation.

Marty was already a few minutes late, and she wondered if she should take it as a sign to leave immediately. What's the point of more talk with him, she asked herself disgustedly. What's the point of meaningless convention if it makes you unhappy, came a retort from her psyche.

"What's life for, if you can't enjoy it?" came a completely new voice.

Bliss turned towards the voice and saw Marty smiling down at her. "You read my mind," she answered drily, and refused to return his good humor.

"You look very beautiful, despite your frown," he said simply.

Bliss was aware of a familiar chill as once more she was caught between her desire and her morality. "You're trying to simplify an impossible dilemma," she challenged him immediately. "I can't see any worthwhile purpose for our meeting."

"So why did you come?"

"I'm weak," she answered quietly.

"Look Bliss, I don't believe our situation is completely hopeless. True there are complexities, but they can be handled."

"What about right and wrong?"

"What about beauty?"

"Any beauty here stems from your adultery, and I refuse to keep on being a part of it. Why should I expect my adolescent son to respect anything I ever taught him, when I'm willing to throw away my values for the sake of your convenience?"

Marty didn't even bother to respond to what was obviously a losing argument, and simply reverted to completely boyish behavior throwing himself at her mercy, "Bliss, maybe it is wrong in all the rule books, but I don't want to let you go. Look at me. I'm young with you. When we're together I don't cough, sneeze, wheeze or choke. I'm happy. Doesn't that count for something?"

"Would you actually divorce your wife for me?" she blurted out and hated herself for asking. Her face grew red, and she turned away from him in shame at what sounded like begging.

"I would," he answered in a voice he didn't quite recognize as his own.

"I don't believe you," she answered, focusing her eyes on the El in the distance.

He moved to caress her and she dodged him.

"Please don't turn away from me, Bliss. We both know this isn't easy. I do care for you, but I need space to work things out."

"Then take all the space you want and leave me alone. You're making me feel cheap."

"Why?"

"Because I don't like the role I'm in."

"Bliss," he said softly, "life isn't always black and white."

"You're right. It's more like the abusers and the abused."

"Do you feel like I'm abusing you?"

"Actually, I feel like you're using me."

"Bliss, I just told you I'm trying to work something out for us."

"What you're telling me is that you're about to make two women feel like shit—your wife and me."

"I didn't know you were so concerned about my wife," he said sarcastically."

"Marty," Bliss finally softened, "I'm concerned about this whole mess. It's wrong for all of us."

Slowly, they left the boardwalk and began walking towards the water. The salty air intoxicated Marty, as it mingled with his hair and filled his lungs. He began to feel in control of the situation, and told himself that everything would work out. "Let's get our feet wet," he urged Bliss, and stooped to take off his shoes and socks.

Bliss took hers off, but didn't move to follow him. "Marty, I still don't know where I stand with you," she said.

"Why not? Don't you trust me?"

"Marty, that's just it," yelled Bliss above the crashing waves. "I don't. You were perfectly happy to stay married to your wife and keep me on a string. And now, just because I pressured you, you tell me you'll divorce her. How can I possibly believe you?"

Marty ignored her logic and pulled her toward the water. Although she let herself be dragged along, Bliss continued to argue, but changed her tactics.

"Marty, ever since Chaim Katz, the yeshiva student, visited my apartment, I can't stop thinking about good and evil."

"It's a valid subject," he agreed, glad they were no longer speaking directly about his marriage.

"Do you think there's evil in the world?" she asked as they jogged in the surf.

"Quite possibly."

"Then how can you deny right and wrong?"

"Concepts of right and wrong are often the figments of subjective middle class convention, which are used as a bludgeon to oppress free thought. Conversely, good and evil are universal symbols for high and low aspects of human behavior."

"You're very abstract," said Bliss. "I want to know if you think evil is an entity that actually exists in the world?"

"Why?"

"Because I'm afraid of it. I think evil may be a seductive process that happens gradually and feels good." By now they were up to their knees in the surf and the sky was blackening.

"You make it sound exciting. Why are you so afraid?" joked Marty and pulled her further into the sea.

"Look at the way we met," persisted Bliss. "If not for your wife, I wouldn't know you."

"True," Marty answered very quietly.

"At the time, I thought it was a great coincidence. I fooled myself into thinking it was my destiny from providence. Now I'm not sure what it was."

"You mean you think it was evil," laughed Marty, splashing her.

"It's cold," she screeched, but she was actually glad he didn't seem to take her fears seriously. She really wanted him to convince her the relationship was O.K., and she splashed him back.

"It's good to have fun," he yelled, and threw even more water on her.

"Don't you ever get scared that you're wrong?" she finally laughed.

"I've been wrong too much to scare easily," he joked, but then he looked at her very seriously. "Sometimes you scare me."

"You mean the way I get mad at you?"

"That's only part of it."

"What's the other part?" she asked, trickling water on his neck.

"You want so much. I don't know if I could ever satisfy you."

"Sometimes the need becomes a physical ache," she acknowledged in deadly quiet.

"I too have a need," continued Marty. "For a number of years, I ignored it or tried to satisfy myself through work. But now I want to explore my craving, and find out where it comes from and where it goes." He stopped and pointed directly over the ocean. "See that blackness out there?"

"Mm hm," she answered, intrigued that his fascination with the darkness matched her own.

"It's infinite," he said, with growing passion. "There's no power greater than that swelling darkness. If only we could harness it." The sound of the waves enhanced his ardor and he hugged her tightly. "I've never admitted this to anyone Bliss, but I want some of that power. I want to make an impact as great as the magnitude of a spectacular wave crashing into the bottom of the sea."

"Corny, but I like it," smiled Bliss. "Maybe it's because I'm soaking wet."

"I'm talking about something beyond all known comprehension," continued Marty, as if he never heard Bliss. His speech was hypnotic, and Marty was filled with an overwhelming intensity to express hidden passion. He tore off his shirt and began beating his chest rhythmically. "I'm 52 years old and I'm a survivor. I've survived a career, a marriage and a kid. And now I'm finally in love...I'm a sensual, sexual, beautiful, erotic male," he bellowed, "and I want every star in the sky to bear witness to that."

"Marty, there's a huge wave coming," yelled Bliss. "Head back for shore."

But it took several moments for her words to penetrate Marty's reverie, and he was caught up by the wave.

On shore, Bliss watched him fight to get back to land, and glimpsed his vulnerability for the first time. Marty was completely spent when he finally reached her, and threw himself on the sand. "Bliss I love you," he whispered. "There was never any love for me before yours."

Bliss knelt beside him. "I love you too, Marty," she breathed very softly, her head on his chest and her legs stretched against his in the sand and surf.

He scooped up a handful of sand mixed with water. "This is good Bliss, not evil. Feel the texture," he said and began to drip the mixture into her palm..

"That feels wonderful," said Bliss and kissed him.

"Isn't it great the way water holds sand together," said Marty gently. "It holds things together just like we're together."

Bliss enjoyed his unabashed tenderness, and allowed herself to share in the warmth of his satisfaction.

Later, Marty and Bliss drove home in silence. Each privately wondered how their fantasy would fulfill itself. Bliss occupied her racing brain with the droplets of rain that fell on Marty's windshield. The wipers mesmerized both of them and enhanced intimate feelings. Marty's arm around her shoulder made her believe they belonged together, and almost lulled her into sleep. All her previous fears and objections forgotten, she mumbled contentedly into his hand, "Let's make our dreams come true."

"Dreams, the stuff that life is made of," Marty free associated. Still drunk on the salty air, he continued. "I never even knew this dream existed."

"Which dream?"

"The dream that makes your heart feel like it's home."

His words moved her because they expressed her own feelings. "I think I've changed, Marty." she said quietly. "I don't think I'll ever scream again."

"Good, we'll save on analysis," he joked.

"But do you think we'll ever really have a home?" she asked, and the first shadow crossed her face.

CHAPTER 31

"Good Morning, The Salon, Judi speaking. How may I help you?"

"Hi, this is Anne Zemmel. I need to change my appointment this week."

"You're with Phil, right?"

"Mm hm."

"When would you like to come in?"

"This Thursday around 2:00 would be good."

"O.K. Mrs. Zemmel, I'm just going to put you on hold while I confirm that for you."

Anne expected to listen to the usual musak, and was surprised, when instead she heard voices. She was about to inform whoever was on the other end that the wires were crossed, but at that moment she heard her own name mentioned and kept silent.

"...Anne Zemmel."

"How delicious. Tell me."

"While she's out trying to save the world, her husband's out screwing around."

Anne froze. She wanted to strangle the voice on the other end, yet she could do nothing but listen for more.

"That's interesting, but how can you be sure? Give me some particulars."

Just then the connection broke, and the receptionist was back on the line.

"Mrs. Zemmel?"

"Yes," whispered Anne, her cheeks flaming.

"Thursday's fine."

Anne hung up the phone with rigid fingers. All her previous suspicions about Marty glared at her. But she admitted to herself that her thoughts were actually more than suspicions. She was really sure of the truth. The only difference was that now her fears were confirmed by others, and she was infuriated by the shame of humiliation.

More than their words, she heard the glee of the voices on the phone; their cynicism about what was important to her. It's like they want to see me dragged in the mud, thought Anne. My humiliation is their entertainment. And Marty doesn't give a damn. He didn't even bother to inform me of my new role as cast off. I'm so dispensable to his life, he didn't need to let me know it, she seethed.

Just then, a woman's face jogged Anne's memory. I know it, she thought. But from where? It doesn't connect to the voice on the phone. This woman is very sad, continued Anne and realized the face was from a recent dream. The woman was in a lot of pain and we were talking. This must have something to do with Marty.

Relax and let the associations come, she actually seemed to hear Marty. It's ironic that he should be the guide to his own betrayal, Anne laughed bitterly to herself.

Describe her face, continued the voice.

It's very unhappy, sagging. with bags under her eyes. Maybe she was pretty once, but not anymore.

Where is this woman?

On a plane. I'm on it too.

Why did you stop?, asked Marty's voice.

Shut up, asshole. I need a drink.

I thought you wanted to find out more about your dream, coaxed the voice. Is this woman alone?

She's got three children, but they're not with her. She's divorced. Her ex-husband's also a doctor.

Is he a shrink too?

No, an orthopedist...When I hear she's divorced, I get nauseous. I start sweating. The woman stares at me.

What's the matter with you, she asks. You look pale.

I'm scared, I tell her. I think you're me.

She doesn't seem at all surprised, so I keep talking. We're both 52 and kind of look alike. We're even married to doctors.

But mine's an orthopedist. He's very rich, says the woman.

So what, I answer. They both betrayed us.

Dream and reality merged for Anne at that moment. She was sure she was going to be sick. This is killing me. You're killing me, she wanted to scream at Marty. You're making me eat myself up alive. You should be going through this hell, not me.

But Marty wasn't there. Anne couldn't grab him, and throw him to the floor and stomp him to death. Nor could she chop him into small pieces, and throw them into the sewer where he belonged. So she did what was convenient. She went to her cabinet for some scotch.

Don't you think it's a little early for that, came Marty's voice once more.

How dare you pretend to care whether I drink or not you damned hypocrite, Anne raged inwardly, pouring her scotch and belting it down. Where's the plane going, continued her nemesis.

How the hell do I know, you fuck, she almost screamed. Go ask yourself if you're so interested. But you can't, can you? Cause it's my dream, not yours, and we don't share a life anymore. We don't even have a facade for the neighbors.

But the question was unavoidable and she wondered where the plane was going.

To Israel, she finally answered herself.

Where in Israel?

Look, it was only a dream. I really don't know...

We were going to Jerusalem, she eventually continued. To a conference in the Old City. We were exploring our heritage.

So you were dreaming about your identity, reasoned the voice.

Perhaps, she sighed, calmed by the drink. The woman who I think was me was crying. She didn't think there could be life after divorce.

186

And what do you think?

I think I like my life the way it is or thought it was. The passion's gone, but I've forgotten what it was like. I don't even miss it...But I guess you do, she realized, feeling a little high. That's what's driving you to abandon me. You don't even care that I have to hear the gossip about myself when I call to make an appointment at the salon. You've shattered me, Marty. Do you realize that? Will you accept responsibility? But Marty's voice was gone. There was only dead silence.

She reached for the scotch, poured herself a double and no longer cared what time it was. The phone rang and she remembered her luncheon date with her son.

Allen never returned home to live for very long periods of time after he graduated from college. He and Marty always found their relationship close to impossible, but when Allen announced his plans to become a free lance writer, the gap widened even further. Marty always assumed his son would be a doctor despite their stormy relationship. He believed Allen's choice was out of pure spite, and took it as an open sign of his son's hostility.

Despite the fact that Allen gained some success in his field and seemed happier than in his earlier years, the animosity between father and son didn't diminish. Allen and Marty were still unable to remain in a room for more than 15 minutes without a blow up.

Not surprisingly, Allen refused to meet his mother at home, so they chose a deli close to his New York apartment where they renewed their relationship every few months. Both believed they shared a telepathy that related to the wounds Marty inflicted on them, and Allen particularly admired Anne's strength in enduring the horror of Marty's closed personality. The only thing he couldn't understand was why his mother continued to live with his father.

As an adult, Allen spent endless hours raging at a shrink because he felt he never had a father who truly cared about him, and would often become abusive to the shrink just for being a shrink. He also enjoyed venting his bitterness by writing pieces that exposed the mental health profession.

Allen considered his visits with his Mom very important and did his best never to cancel their luncheon dates. But today a major magazine needed him to do a piece immediately, and he was reluctantly calling to take a rain check. As soon as he heard her voice, he knew his timing was not good.

"Ma, Ma are you there?"

"Yes Allen. I'm here."

"What's wrong?"

"Nothing...everything."

"What's that supposed to mean?"

Anne felt clamped in a vice. She wanted to blurt everything out to her son in a long wail, but she wouldn't allow herself the freedom. Instead she continued to talk in circles.

"I had a strange dream last night. I was on a plane to Israel with a woman I thought was me."

"Ma, why are you so cryptic this morning? What's going on?"

"And the woman was getting divorced."

"Oh...It's you and Dad," he said with little surprise in his voice.

"I really can't talk about it," said Anne's outer voice, while her inner voice clamored for recognition.

"Ma, you sound very upset. I guess my timing is really off, but I can't meet you for lunch today. Is that going to be a problem?"

Yes, she wanted to scream. That is a problem. I really need to talk to you. There's nothing in this whole damned world I can count on.

But she said nothing, so Allen continued.

I hate letting you down like this. Maybe we can meet next week...Oh no, I can't. I'm going to be in Ohio. I'll make it as soon as I can."

"I know you will," said Anne's brave voice. "Today wouldn't be such a good day anyway. I really look a wreck." But inside she was crying so hard she barely heard Allen's voice.

"Why are you feeling so bad...? Ma, do you hear me?"

"I really can't talk about this over the phone."

"Well, whatever he did, that bastard's not worth your aggravation."

"He's all I've got."

"How can you say that? You've got friends, charities. What about me, Ma? Do you call me nothing?"

"Allen, I thought he and I shared some respect and trust. Now I realize it's all been a farce. I tried to make us feel like a real family, but it never really worked. There was always something missing."

"His love, Ma," said Allen quietly. "He never had anything for anybody."

"Except his patients," complained Anne bitterly. "He's a miracle worker in the hospital."

"You sound like me," said Allen. "Try to relax."

"You sound like him...I'm sorry dear, that wasn't fair of me."

"Are you sure it's O.K., Ma?" asked Allen once more.

Her entire body contorted into a spasm of helplessness. She wanted to yell and cry about Marty's betrayal. She wanted Allen to be near her to listen to her frustration. But, as before, she said nothing, and Allen read her silence as an assurance that everything was under control.

Anne hung up the phone and looked for Lillie in the kitchen. We're having steak tonight," said Anne. "If I'm late, tell Dr. Zemmel to start without me."

"O.K. Mrs. Zemmel."

"Thanks, Lillie. I'm going out now."

Lillie nodded quietly and watched Anne walk out the door. She continued to stare in Anne's direction for several moments. She wasn't surprised to see her blasted, but never before did Lillie see Anne leave the house with absolutely no makeup.

CHAPTER 32

The classroom was the same and the kids were mostly the same, but there was a major difference. It wasn't school anymore. At least for a while, the school format was changed. Andi was excited by the newness of the prospect and she was pleased that the new doctor wasn't actually a doctor. He was a psychologist. Also, Sam, as everyone called him, was much cuter than Dr. Zemmel.

At the moment all eyes were on Tina, who for once wasn't sure what to say. Everyone was challenged by the question, "Why are you here?" This was particularly difficult for Tina because her psychiatrist was urging her to go home for at least a weekend and she was afraid. "Because I want to be," she finally answered.

"That's a start," commented the therapist. "Remember, there are no right answers, just honest or dishonest ones. O.K. Yolanda, why are you here?"

"That's the same thing I want to know," the girl grumbled good naturedly. "You kinda cute for a white boy, Sam, but I'm sick of having my brain picked."

"O.K., that's a fair comment," said Sam Haddad as he leaned back on his folding chair and loosened his tie. "You guys are part of my program.

"Your what?" asked Yolanda incredulously.

"He's talking about his college experiment," announced Tina in an attempt to recover her leadership position. "Every once in a while, the outside decides to study screwballs."

"Hold on," said Haddad, visibly unsure of what to say next.

"Stop trying to bullshit us," interjected Mouth, "you know we're screwy."

"I'm glad to hear your opinion Mouth," countered Haddad. "But I'm not here to study you and I don't think you're screwy." He was about to say more about the various aspects of craziness, but stopped himself. Who was he to argue with kids who'd been told they were loony for years? They'd see through him in a minute, as some obviously already had. He wanted to help them feel good about themselves, and telling them their perceptions were wrong was certainly not the way to go about it.

The kids sensed his hesitation and eagerly awaited his next move. Underneath their anxiety, they shared Andi's hope. Maybe this guy could help.

"Actually, I'm here to have fun with you," said Haddad, "to set up a gym program. We'll do some yoga and other indoor activities, as well as do something outside."

He immediately noticed anxiety on their faces and realized he was moving too fast. The thought of the outside obviously terrified them. "We won't go outside until you feel ready," he assured them. "This is a step-by-step program. But before we can do anything, we need to continue getting to know each other. Each of us will say something we want the group to know, starting with the word, `I'. Like this...I'm a Palestinian studying to be a psychologist at Columbia University and I love working with kids...O.K. Carlos, let's hear from you."

"I'm here," said Carlos noncommittally.

"Good," said Haddad, "you're on the right track. Tina, be next."

"I'm afraid to go home," came from a new voice within her.

"Thanks, Tina. Jerry, what about you?"

"I am the greatest."

"Yolanda..."

"I am too fat."

"Mouth..."

"I'm the meanest and the ugliest."

"You're next Andi."

"I'm crying," whispered Andi, "and I don't even know why."

The group was momentarily stunned, but Haddad pulled her through, "Sometimes a good, warm feeling makes you bleary eyed. Don't worry, as long as your mascara isn't running," he joked in a friendly way.

Andi began giggling in spite of herself. Once more, everyone stared. Haddad wondered why she was losing control and attempted to focus her. "Is it my suspenders?" he asked, "Or just me?"

"You're...you're just so different from Dr. Zemmel," gasped Andi. "He hardly ever talks and you stand there and bellow at us."

"Yeah," added Yolanda. "You sound like a moose."

"Where's your space ship, Sam," asked Jerry.

"Same place as yours," Carlos finally joked.

"I'll tell you all about my spaceship," said Haddad, anxious to gain acceptance, "as soon as you move to the blue mats on the floor. We're going to do some jumping jacks."

Haddad wasn't completely surprised when nobody moved. In fact, he was prepared for it. He simply met them eyeball to eyeball, "What's wrong with jumping jacks?"

"That's not yoga," objected Tina.

"You're right! This is the warm up. Now get going!"

The strength of his voice was invigorating, and soon they were all jumping on the mats.

"And now for the yoga portion; the sun exercise. In fact, let's do it to music," he said, and immediately inserted an upbeat disc. "It's simple, just follow me. But first, let's get some sun." It was a surprise to see all the brightness when Haddad raised the shades. "Stand with your face toward the sun and your hands clasped in front of you," he directed.

The group was motivated by a sense of intrigue and clumsily followed him through a series of stretches with a variety of ups and downs. They repeated the mildly strenuous exercise four times before he allowed them to rest.

"Super. As you grow stronger, I'll raise the challenge. Soon you'll do ten each morning. Now roll over to somebody else's mat. That's right. Get into pairs."

Andi grew tense when she found Tina next to her. "Why are you crying?" whispered Tina.

"What do you care," mumbled Andi, mad at herself for answering.

"Are you still mad at me?"

"What do you think? I trusted you and found out you're a creep."

"Let's go girls, keep up with us," intruded Haddad's strident voice. "We're forming a caterpillar."

Soon they were undulating across the floor on all fours with Haddad at the head. Middle Eastern belly dancing music played in the background.

"Where we going?" yelled Jerry.

"Who cares! I like this," yelled Carlos in the loudest voice he ever used.

"Chug-a-chug-a choo-choo," screeched Yolanda.

Andi jumped at the tug on her leg. "I'm sorry," whispered Tina.

"You don't know how to be sorry. The only one you love is yourself."

"Look Andi, I only..."

"You only made me feel like you cared, and then let me know you didn't."

"I didn't think you would take me so seriously."

"That's cause you know you're a liar. I didn't find out till it was too late."

"Watch out," yelled Yolanda, "we're heading for the wall."

"The wall, great," screamed Mouth. "Let's smash it!"

And in a sense, they did. Arms, legs and butts jammed into the wall and then everyone lay in a laughing heap. There was a new lightness and the group seemed more like kids than patients.

"You're laughing," said Haddad, "and that's my mission. I think every kid should be able to laugh. Now, let's form a circle in the middle of the room."

Everyone headed for the center except Andi and Tina. They were so deeply involved in their conversation that they were unaware of the others, who were beginning to stare at them.

"I lied because I was scared," said Tina.

"Of what?"

"That you would reject me," answered Tina, raising her voice.

"Rejection, rejection," bleated Mouth in a taunting sing-song voice.

Tina and Andi froze at his words. Their faces turned beet red as they remembered the rest of the group. The nakedness of the moment seared Andi, and she wished again that she never heard of Tina.

But then she heard Haddad's voice, which was becoming a life preserver. "Rejection hurts," he commented, "and the saddest part is that sometimes fear of rejection causes us to push away those we would often like to get close to."

"Hey, where'd all the fun go?" complained Jerry. "You're starting to sound just like the shrinks."

"Shut up," countered Carlos. "Rejection is my favorite topic."

"Jerry," continued Haddad, "rejection is part of our lives. Maybe that's why we're talking about it right now. It's unavoidable."

"Yeah!" interjected Yolanda. "I thought those two were my friends," she motioned towards Tina and Andi, "but they're off in a corner whispering."

Haddad was aware of a deepening negativity, and worked to combat it.

"The key is to deal with rejection effectively, so that it doesn't destroy our self image," he interjected. "We will explore new ways of confronting old hurts so that we make sure we don't stop liking ourselves."

"Nobody really wants to be my friend," responded Tina, very moved by Haddad's words.

"Maybe that's because you're always trying to manipulate us," answered Yolanda. "I like you Tina, but I hate your bossiness."

"I like you Tina," added Carlos, "but I don't think you ever really see me."

"Let's make a circle around Tina," directed Haddad. "Come here, Tina, and sit in the middle. Remember, these kids care enough about you to speak honestly. It may be a little hard to take at first, but I think you can handle it."

Slowly, they regrouped around Tina. "Before we speak," counseled Haddad, "remember, every word counts. Everything we say will have a huge effect on someone in the group."

It was very quiet and Andi was the first to speak, "You're different from anyone I've ever known, Tina. Since I've been in the hospital, I've discovered a lot of confusion inside myself and somehow you've become a part of it. You hurt me the other night in your room, but maybe it's because I didn't really take you into consideration. I only saw myself as vulnerable and didn't think I could ever really make an impact on anyone else."

"Does that mean you're willing to give me a second chance," asked Tina hopefully.

"I guess so, but I'm going to be a lot smarter about things this time."

"What does that mean?" asked Haddad.

His question embarrassed Andi. She was near very personal feelings and everyone was listening. Yet, she wanted to sort through the complex maze, and so she forged ahead.

"I was dumb enough to think I loved Tina."

"That is dumb," agreed Mouth.

"But I was confusing love with something else," continued Andi, despite the comment. "It wasn't Tina I was reaching for so much as a part of myself that I saw in her."

"So you were really loving you," whispered Yolanda.

"That's what Dr. Zemmel said."

"And what do you say?" asked Haddad.

"I also think I was beginning to love a part of myself that I never knew existed."

"So then I never really hurt you," offered Tina.

"Maybe not," laughed Andi for the first time, "but it sure felt like it."

Once more laughter was healing.

Yolanda was encouraged to be forthright, "I'm glad you two are so tight, but what about me?"

Tina and Andi were so wrapped up in each other, they had forgotten about Yolanda and now all they could do was stare at her. Their silence hurt Yolanda as much as excuses. "I should have known better than to trust white people" she said shortly.

"Please don't talk like that," said Andi.

"Why not? It's true, ain't it?"

"Don't talk mean to her or she'll cry," quipped Mouth.

Haddad didn't like the destructive energy of the conversation and tried to focus it more therapeutically. "Listen up gang," he called, "our next exercise is standing on our heads."

But they didn't pay the slightest attention to him. Instead, all eyes turned to Andi whose temper was rising. "Hey guys, stop putting words in my mouth and analyzing me," she said hotly. "I'm sorry I hurt your feelings, Yolanda, and that you felt left out. But it's not because I'm white. I resent that."

"Well maybe I resent being ignored after I thought we were friends," answered Yolanda just as heatedly.

"Look, I said I was sorry. What do you want?"

"A little respect would be nice. And that's something white folks always forget when it comes to us."

"It's my fault Yolanda," volunteered Tina, "Don't blame her."

"You white too."

"True," agreed Tina, "Maybe you're right. But whatever it is, we're sorry. Won't you forgive us?"

"Hmm..."

"Come on Yolanda, don't be angry," begged Andi. "I like you a lot. I'm sorry that you think I'm a racist, because I don't mean to be. But no matter what, I know your friendship is very important to me."

"Gee, you sound corny," said Carlos, "but I like it."

"This is nothin' but a looney bin," asserted Mouth.

"And you're all crazy," Yolanda finally laughed, "but I guess I'll forgive you...this time."

And then the three girls were hugging each other, only to be interrupted by Jerry and Mouth's heckling.

Haddad was in awe of the dialogue that transpired. He never expected to hear such an honest and lucid conversation on American racism come from this group. His respect for the kids escalated. But when he saw the boys teasing the girls, he was afraid things might fall apart and immediately diverted them to a physical exercise.

"Everyone get to a mat." he boomed. "In about two seconds I want to see you doing headstands. By the way, when I get hospital clearance for each of you, we're going on a hike." As soon as the words were out of his mouth, he was afraid he made a mistake. The last time he mentioned outdoors, there was definite tension.

But they all scuffled to the mats without further complaints, and Haddad was convinced that these kids had more on the ball than anyone realized.

Helping Yolanda's feet into the air, Andi wondered why the girl was really in the hospital. She knew Yolanda didn't think she belonged there, and Andi admitted that Yolanda seemed saner than anyone else. When Yolanda was finally balanced on her head, Andi remembered Yolanda never got any visitors or care packages.

"Look at me, I'm standing on my head," screeched Yolanda and all 200 pounds of her shook.

"Super," bellowed Haddad.

"Aren't you going to say something, Andi?" demanded Yolanda.

"I'm sorry," said Andi.

"That's all you ever say lately," complained Yolanda. What's wrong with you?"

"I was just wondering why no one ever comes to see you," blurted Andi. Yolanda's feet slumped to the floor and Andi wished she could take back her words. "I didn't mean to ask," she gasped.

"It's O.K.", breathed Yolanda. "It ain't your fault that no one gives a damn about me."

"Do you mean you can't go home when you get better?"

"When I get better," laughed Yolanda bitterly. "I told you all along there wasn't nothin' wrong with me in the first place. They just don't want me. All the social worker is doing is trying to place me."

"Place you?"

"Yeah...like in a foster home."

"Hey Yolanda," Andi suddenly brightened. "Maybe you can live with us. I hate being an only child."

"Andi, you don't know nothin'."

"About what?"

"About white people."

"Are you starting that again?" asked Andi, getting annoyed.

"I never started anything," insisted Yolanda stubbornly. "White people did."

"Well my parents aren't like that."

"Oh really. You think they want big black me in their little white neighborhood?"

Andi started to open her mouth and closed it. Yolanda just looked knowingly, while Andi finally got the point. They stared at each other really hard.

"It's my turn to stand on my head," Andi finally said. "I'm scared. I never did this before."

"Close your eyes. That's what I did and then it was fun... So I guess that's the end of your offer," ventured Yolanda, grabbing Andi's legs.

"I never said that, you did. You're probably right about my parents. They didn't like Joe 'cause he wasn't Jewish. But I didn't let that stop me. We saw each other all the time and he was always in my house."

"But he didn't live there."

"True, but he had his own home. You say you don't."

Yolanda wanted to punch Andi because her words sounded cruel. But then she realized the girl didn't mean to hurt her. She was just trying to help.

"Andi, I already have one social worker I can't stand. Just drop it. Kick your legs up a little more and you'll be standing on your head."

The world looked upside down to Andi and it was not as bad as she thought. The new perspective actually helped her to see things from Yolanda's point of view. She realized she wanted to make everything all right for Yolanda, but knew she couldn't. Yolanda's pretty sharp, she thought. If I asked Mom and Dad to bring her home, they'd probably lock me up all over again.

As Andi's legs came down, she saw Yolanda's eyes were smiling and was grateful her friend wasn't angry. Andi smiled back.

"Thanks for the offer anyway," said Yolanda. It's the best one I've had."

CHAPTER 33

"I'm afraid of everything," complained Andi in her next session with Zemmel.

"By that you mean your feelings," he surmised.

"Maybe...I'm drawing you another picture."

"Andi, you never talk about your creativity."

"You mean the way I like to draw?"

"Mm hum."

"What's there to say? I like to draw. It's no big deal."

"I didn't ask you to evaluate it, Andi, just talk about it."

"Drawing makes me feel powerful."

"I liked what you did with the colors in the picture you gave me."

"I was thinking about you when I drew it."

Zemmel said nothing, but motioned for her to continue.

"I was thinking about how much I liked talking to you."

"Is it just talking to me Andi or the things we talk about?"

"What we talk about. There's freedom here to say things...that I really can't talk about anywhere else."

"When you draw, you take that freedom of expression upon yourself and create space for it."

"But I can't always draw. I have trouble coping with the really hard feelings...like when I slit my wrists...I was totally lost. I couldn't hold all that despair inside, alone. I needed expression, even if it was killing myself."

"So your suicide attempt was a very negative expression. You had to do something to get the feelings out, even if it was at the expense of your own body."

"There was this huge block of frustration that was thrashing inside me the night I cut myself. I couldn't bear living with it."

"The power you're describing reminds me of your drawing."

"That power drives me crazy," exclaimed Andi. "Like when I first came to the hospital. I was very trapped and angry. I was mad that I wasn't dead. I didn't want to face another minute of life."

"You were overwhelmed by the powerful feelings. It felt like craziness."

"Actually, I was secretly happy to be in a place where I could really go crazy," confided Andi. "I was sick of pretending to be normal."

"Give us some details about how you acted out the frustration in the hospital."

"On the first day, when the nurse wouldn't let me use the phone to call Joe, I went insane. Something went off inside me and all I could do was bash my head against the wall." Andi stopped abruptly.

"Go on," urged Zemmel.

"It hurt when I was finally able to call Joe and he wouldn't talk to me," whispered Andi in a voice close to tears. "It hurt so much I couldn't face it. I was sure Joe would care when he heard where I was. I pinned all my hopes on him. But when he refused to come to the phone, I knew I meant nothing to him. And without him, I was nothing. There was no point to my life. It was too much for me to bear, so I blocked out everything. And the next thing I knew I was throwing pies."

"The violence was an antidote to insufferable hurt," Zemmel almost said to himself. "But even that stems from your need to express what's important to you. And when all avenues are blocked, a kind of maddening frustration kicks in that can escalate to violence."

"I don't understand you," said Andi, and she was kind of glad she didn't. Whatever he said sounded awful.

"I'm sorry," said Zemmel smiling. "Your anger is a method of dealing with the hurt. But it's also a way of expressing what you have trouble putting into words. And that's where I think your creativity lies."

"You mean whenever someone makes me feel like shit, I get mad so it doesn't hurt so much."

"Right."

"I get that part, but I don't see what it has to do with creativity."

"You need to express yourself in terms of deeper feelings. When this happens positively, through drawing, we call it art. But when it happens explosively, we call it madness. Yet the strength and power of either expression stems from the same source...your creativity."

"You make it sound like I could go either way. Like I have a split personality."

"I didn't mean to scare you," said Zemmel. "The idea is to give that creative part of yourself a chance to speak with a new voice and to stop punishing it."

"I like when we talk about loving myself rather than hating myself," said Andi.

"You can't love yourself till you know what it is that you preserve and protect by hating yourself."

"I preserve the idea that I don't need love as much as I actually do."

"Because you don't deserve it?" asked Zemmel.

"Because I'm afraid I'll never have a loving relationship with anyone," confided Andi very quietly.

"Especially your mother," agreed Zemmel. "Worse, still, you'll never get past self destructive behavior."

Andi stared at him helplessly. "What am I supposed to do?" she asked in a stunned voice.

"Stop using anger and hate as a way to block off your need for love."

"Should I tell my mother that I love her?"

"Mm."

"It's hard for me to say that when she doesn't love me the way I want to be loved. Sometimes she makes my whole body ache."

"Can you tell her about the ache you have for her love?"

"I'm afraid to. She never sees me."

"Then we'll have to work hard at getting her to see you. We can start by using your positive feelings to overcome her negativity. I know it's risky for you, but love is never without risk."

* * * *

Andi instinctively looked for Mary once she was outside Zemmel's office. She wanted to tell her what a great session they had, when she remembered Mary was gone. No one ever sticks around, Andi lamented to herself.

It was raining and the darkness increased the institutional gloom. What's the point of all this openness, when it only leaves you drained and empty, thought Andi.

"I know it's hard to bridge the gap between the inside of a shrink's office and the outside world," came a voice she couldn't quite place, and then Andi realized it was Sherrine's, her new nurse.

Sherrine MacIntyre was attractively dark and intense. She was intrigued by Andi's history and anxious to win her confidence. But all her attempts at friendliness were met by resentment from Andi, who hated Sherrine for not being Mary.

So the two walked back to Andi's cot in silence. Sherrine sat down in the chair, while Andi crawled onto her cot and faced the wall. The good feelings from her visit with Zemmel appeared gone, when a surprising thought entered her consciousness. I wish he was in my family, she thought. Almost in spite of herself, she turned to Sherrine. "I want Dr. Zemmel to be my mother," she said.

"That's not so unusual," responded Sherrine in her most neutral tone. "Mothering is often an important part of therapy."

"But he's a man," questioned Andi. "Why would I think of him as my mother?"

"Sympathy and affirmation feel good whether they come from a man or a woman."

"I guess I used to think of Mary as my mother or the way I wanted my mother to be."

Sherrine was glad for the opportunity to penetrate the barrier between herself and Andi, so she asked about Mary. "Would you like to talk about missing her?"

But Andi was tired of opening up to people who continually disappeared. "Don't psyche me out," she said in a tone that she immediately knew was too harsh. "You wouldn't understand."

"Try me."

"Mary always listened, even when I was off the wall. She helped me realize that healing is possible."

"Healing's a process that takes a lot of time and patience. It also takes a lot of love."

"That's why I think of Dr. Zemmel as my mother. I want him to love me."

"What about your own mother, Andi? Can't you enjoy a relationship with her?"

"I don't think my mother understands this process."

"Hmm," said Sherrine.

"Dr. Zemmel just told me I should start telling my mother I love her, but I'm not too sure about it."

"Hmm," Sherrine repeated herself.

"Would you stop saying that," laughed Andi in spite of herself. "You sound like a shrink."

"Maybe they should give me a bigger paycheck," smiled Sherrine.

"They should pay me too, just for staying in this gloomy jailhouse."

Tension finally broke. Andi was glad that someone shared her sense of humor. "You're really funny," she laughed.

"So are you Andi. But seriously, maybe you wouldn't have to stay in this jailhouse that much longer if you and your mother would give each other a chance. Your chart looks pretty positive." Andi stared at her nurse in shock. This was the first time, since she came to the hospital, that anyone even mentioned going home. But if it involved getting along with her mother, she wasn't too hopeful.

"It's pretty rough between us," she muttered.

"Do you know she's been working with one of Dr. Zemmel's associates?" asked Sherrine gently.

Andi shook her head. She tried to picture her mother with a shrink, but couldn't.

"They're trying to develop a supportive network for you."

"Why didn't Dr. Zemmel tell me?" asked Andi.

"I'm not sure, but I thought you needed to know."

"It's hard to imagine her being supportive," whispered Andi and fell silent. Somehow the idea of leaving the hospital was just as terrifying as staying.

Sherrine realized that Andi was probably experiencing mixed emotions and didn't wish to upset her, so she also fell silent. Their silence was respectful of one another's feelings. It was the kind of silence that binds people together, rather than estranges them. It promised friendship.

CHAPTER 34

The woods were very quiet and peaceful. Red and gold leaves were still falling. It was such a different world from the institution that Andi dreaded going back. There was Sam's voice again. It was so strident against the dirt and leaves of the path before her, yet it gave the group security. It made them feel that they belonged as much as the trees and pine cones and small pebbles along the way.

"Come on, no stragglers," bellowed Haddad. "We have to keep up the pace."

"I'm tired," groaned Yolanda. "How far we going?"

"It's two miles," said Tina. "We're going all around the lake."

"You been here before?"

"No, I just pay attention."

"Nerd," shot back Yolanda.

"Andi," whispered Tina quietly, "this would be a great place to meet Joe."

"I told you that I'm not sure how I feel about him, and anyway, I wouldn't talk to you about it."

Before they could say anything more, the rest of the group stopped short. Jerry was trembling. His lips quivered, but no sound emerged. Carlos became his voice, "There's a spider crawling up his leg." Everyone stared helplessly at the huge black insect.

Haddad moved faster than Andi imagined anyone could, and was instantly at Jerry's side. His voice was miraculously soothing and Andi thought he reminded her of Zemmel.

"O.K. Jerry," intoned Haddad, "just relax. We'll have it off in a minute."

Andi was surprised at how rigid Jerry's body was as he stood and waited for help. We're just freaks, she suddenly realized, and the warmth disappeared. There was only shame inside.

206

Haddad sensed the discouragement and quickly worked to restore confidence into the group, as he flicked the spider off Jerry's leg. "We're going to have a blind walk," he said. Amidst their grumbling, he put them into pairs, and once again Andi found herself with Tina. Why was this always happening, she wondered.

The rest of the group stood with open mouths as Haddad whipped out a bunch of multicolored scarves from his backpack. He handed one to a member of each pair. "Decide which one of you will be the leader," he instructed them, "and the other one has to put on the blindfold."

"I hate losing control," Tina immediately complained to Andi. "Please let me be the leader first."

"I like darkness," answered Andi, as she put the scarf over her eyes.

Andi actually enjoyed the blindness, although she hated herself for listening to Tina. But soon she forgot about everything, and concentrated on all the sounds and smells of the woods. Wouldn't it be great to just stay here forever, she thought, and never have to worry about relationships again.

"Watch it Andi," shrieked Tina, "there's a tree root."

Andi stumbled, but didn't fall. "You're supposed to let me know what's coming *before* I get there!"

"O.K., switch," directed Haddad.

Why's he always telling us what to do, thought Andi, who really didn't want to take off the blindfold.

"Andi, I'm scared. I can't do this," whined Tina. "I don't like the dark."

"Are you really that scared?" asked Andi, surprised to see Tina so unhinged. Some of her anger at the shivering girl next to her dissipated. "Just try and relax Tina. The dark can be quiet and gentle. You really don't need to be so afraid."

"Well, talk to me then," answered Tina while she reluctantly blindfolded herself.

"About what?"

"My doctor wants me to go home. He says I should at least try an extended visit, but now I'm scared."

"I guess it will be hard to face your friends when they ask where you were," answered Andi, and wondered what she would say to her friends.

"I keep telling you that I don't have any.

Andi stared at Tina. It was as though she heard her for the first time.

"Why not?"

"Nobody I know is on my level."

"You just think you're better than everybody else."

"Maybe I am."

"Or maybe you just push everyone away cause you're scared of them."

"How would you know," hissed Tina.

"I know what you did to me."

The two girls faced each other.

"I am scared," admitted Tina very slowly, "cause I don't have a life out there. My mother wants me to be Miss Perfect. She wants me to have friends, but none of the kids like me. They think I'm a snob cause I don't talk to anyone, but really no one talks to me."

"Maybe cause you're bossy."

"Why?"

"Like Yolanda said, you always try to dominate people."

"Oh really," answered Tina and almost immediately tripped over a rock.

Andi didn't notice and continued berating Tina, "You're constantly telling people what to do and trying to psyche everybody out."

By now, Tina was hopping on one foot. "Ouch, I stubbed my toe," she screamed.

But Andi still paid no attention, because she was so involved in her diatribe against Tina, "When it's time for you to give, you push everyone away. So in the end, nobody wants to be your friend."

Rather than answer, Tina sat down in the middle of the path and cradled her foot. Suddenly, she was laughing hysterically.

Andi stood over her, helplessly wide eyed. Is Tina insane, she asked herself. Is this my fault? She stooped down to remove Tina's blindfold, but the girl stood up too soon and began running with the blindfold still in place.

"Andi," yelled Tina, "that's how friends talk. You just told me off. No one ever cared enough to do that before. Look at me everyone, I'm not scared anymore. It's fun to be blindfolded in the woods. I'm flying."

The group stood in silent shock, while Tina rammed into a tree. Even Haddad was transfixed. Andi was the first to break the spell. She rushed to Tina.

"Your face is all bloodied. Let's wrap the blindfold around it." And then she and Tina were hugging.

"Sam," screamed Tina, "I'm not scared anymore. I love everyone, even myself. Maybe I'm ready to try a visit home."

Haddad viewed her behavior as manic, but he stuck to his philosophy of building on positives. "Very good Tina," he said, "you're pretty brave. It's a good thing we brought along this emergency ice pack. Let's put it on your face."

"When I do finally leave, I'm going to miss you guys," said Tina to Andi and Yolanda after her face felt better. "Promise that you're not mad at me."

"I'm not mad," said Andi. "I might also be going home for a visit sometime soon."

Yolanda immediately looked down at the ground. Tina and Andi stared at each other. Why were they always forgetting about her? Was Yolanda right, they each wondered privately. Were black people somehow invisible to white people?

"That's if you can believe anything they tell you around here," Andi continued weakly. "I don't even know what they mean by soon."

"You don't have to say that just cause you feel sorry for me," Yolanda whispered.

"She said it cause she cares about you," Tina asserted firmly. "And I do too. The three of us really got tight here. I guess I can't say I don't have friends anymore."

"I don't feel sorry for you, Yolanda," said Andi. "You're the sanest one here. I just want things to work out for you."

"Well maybe they will," said Yolanda. "I don't wanna jinx it, so I didn't say nothin'. But that social worker wrote to an aunt I have in Ohio and she's comin' out next week to talk to me. Who knows? Maybe we'll hit it off."

The girls each went into their private thoughts, and Andi began to enjoy the woods once more. She drew strength from the sky, trees, plants and multicolored leaves.

Her memory reached back to her Period 8 Health Class from last year. The teacher was usually so boring that Andi never paid much attention. That's why she was so surprised to find the class interesting one day. She didn't quite understand what Miss Eng was saying, but it sounded very mysterious. Now the teacher's words echoed in her mind: 'periods of growth are often painful, but they mark a passage.' Am I going through a passage right now, wondered Andi. Will it lead to a magic door? Might the door even be right here in the woods? Will this passage make me feel whole and beautiful?

Last one back's a rotten egg," yelled Yolanda. "Let's race to the road."

Andi was always a slow runner. Orders to run around the track in gym always traumatized her. But now she was filled with a new exhilaration and she actually wanted to run. Yolanda's challenge immediately captured her imagination. "Yahoo," she yelled, "I'm going to beat all of you." And she did.

Life was starting to feel worthwhile.

CHAPTER 35

The group trudged into the ward at twilight. After the sunlit colors of the trees outside, Andi found the fourth floor gloom intolerable. She sensed a controlled, sinister aspect to the green halls, where the mood was tranquilized rather than tranquil. Patients aren't quiet because they want to be, thought Andi. They're quiet because they have to be. Andi flung herself down on her cot and just stared at the wall. She remembered how it looked from a strait jacket, and how she had counted the pieces of blistered paint to keep her sanity. She tried to hold on to the vigor of the race, but it was fading. Going out only made it harder to come back in, she realized. Even this cot feels like a death sentence.

*   *   *   *

A figure in white crept to the next landing of the back steps of the hospital. His breath was getting short. He glanced at the sleeve of the medic's jacket he was wearing. Will the uniform throw them off the track and give me enough time to get to Andi, Joe wondered.

He could hardly believe his recent audacity. What if they catch me? Will it mean a padded cell, electric shock treatment, demented guards pummeling me with rubber hoses? Or will it be like the movie I saw last night where they stashed patients away till even their relatives forgot they existed?

But as the cement steps brought him closer to Andi, Joe's thoughts turned to her. What will Andi look like? Will I be able to handle it? Fearfully, he approached the last stairs to her floor. Real terror developed when he came face to face with the red door that opened up her world to him. What if this is a trap concocted by that nut, Tina? Is this really her floor?

211

Trembling, he placed his hand on the metal and pushed. Will Andi blame me? Will she hate me? Will she even know me? What if I make her worse? His questions steered him through the door and onto the floor. He realized Tina's directions were perfect, when he spotted Andi lying on her cot. Is this really her, he wondered. She looks so thin and fragile.

Andi felt his stare on her and turned. Their eyes met at that moment. She couldn't believe it was Joe. It wasn't possible. He was right there in front of her in flesh and blood; the fantasy turned into reality. She was transfixed.

He saw the look on her face, and was transported to the last night they were together. Andi was full of expectation—all prepared with her birth control and sexy smile. He was supposed to be her Prince Charming. She wanted him to make perfect love to her, to give her a total orgasm.

But he knew it was all wrong for him. It was a farce, a lie. How could he possibly fulfill her fantasies that night? His own were pretty impossible. He couldn't go through with it and told her to leave. "Let's cool it," he'd said and remembered the tonelessness of his own voice. Andi was so shocked, she didn't say anything. Instead she turned her head in what looked like disgust. He hated the way she looked at him and just wanted to get away, to block out her judgment forever. That look branded him as a failure in his own eyes.

"Joe, where did you get a white uniform?" Andi finally blurted from her cot.

Her question sounded like it came from a great distance, but it brought him back to the present and he sheepishly answered, "My brother's in medical school." And then he grinned, "Pretty clever, huh?"

"Was this Tina's idea?" Andi asked warily, as he sat down on her cot.

"No, she gave me the directions a while ago. But then she told me not to come. She said you didn't really want to see me."

"So why are you here?"

Andi's words were cold, but her voice wasn't, so he decided to tell her what was on his mind. He knew it might sound lame, but he wanted to say it anyway, "I never meant to hurt you."

"Spare me. Anyway, that doesn't answer my question."

"I came because I care about you. Simple as that. No mystery."

Her anger grew with his attempt at simplification, and she desperately searched for words to express her feelings before they got out of control.

"You wouldn't even talk to me on the phone, when I called you out of my complete and utter loneliness. You were the only one I could think of during those first days in this nut house. I was so scared and small, but I was sure you would understand why I hurt so much. I wasn't even angry at you anymore for what happened between us. I was so stupid that I was almost ready to forgive you. And you wouldn't talk to me. You wouldn't even come to the phone."

He accepted her condemnation because he didn't answer her phone call, but he didn't accept her idea that he needed her forgiveness for everything else. It angered him that she felt she had the right to forgive what he perceived as his inability to fulfill her fantasy.

"I'm sorry about the phone call. You're right. I was a jerk. But your being in the hospital was really confusing for me. I was afraid you'd blame me for everything. Like right now— you're ready to forgive me for what you don't even understand."

"Oh, you don't think I know when I'm being kicked out."

"All you see is your own pain. You can't see mine."

"What pain can you possibly have?"

"The pain of having someone very beautiful needing me, and knowing that I have nothing to give."

His honesty struck a deep chord in Andi, and even though her relationship with Joe was humiliating and awkward, she knew it couldn't be ignored. Everything seemed so simple that night, but now she knew it wasn't. She thought of Dr. Zemmel. What would he say about all this added anxiety?

"Is that Tina?" asked Joe quickly, when he spotted a girl motioning wildly to Andi.

"Yeah, that's her. What's she all worked up about?"

"Your parents are here," hissed Tina, running over to Andi's cot.

"What're we gonna do?" whispered Andi.

"You've got to get out of here," announced Tina, who lived for emergencies. "Follow me."

"But Tina, what will they do when they see I'm not here?"

"I've got a plan."

"When don't you," grumbled Andi. "Well what is it then?"

"I'm not sure, but I know something will evolve."

Then she saw the fear in their eyes and added quickly, "O.K. I figured it out. Take those stairs. The ones Joe took to get up here. They lead to the roof. It's really beautiful with trees an plants. Kind of like a penthouse."

"This feels like a passage," muttered Andi to herself.

"What?" asked Tina.

"Nothing. I was just thinking about our hike in the woods."

Andi continued after a pause, "Remember how I said I didn't think I could trust you, Tina."

"Yeah."

"Well, now I know I can. We are friends." The girls hugged quickly.

"Andi, let's go," called Joe, already climbing the stairs two at a time with visions of tranquilizer guns dancing in front of his eyes.

"Tina, what will you tell people when they see I'm missing?" asked Andi in a panic.

"I'll say you hated the hospital and ran back to the woods. That'll throw them off the track for awhile. Be back in half an hour. Do you have a watch?"

"I've got one," called Joe.

"Super," screeched Andi over her shoulder, already following Joe up to the roof. There was a rejuvenation in her spirit that matched the feeling when she won the race, and she immediately vowed that she would never lose it. She would never go into that black hole again. Whatever happened on this visit with Joe, she promised herself she wouldn't fall apart. Her good feelings were too precious to throw away.

Joe reached the top first and let out a low whistle. It was really exquisite. Life wasn't making the kind of sense he expected, but there was a freedom here that he never dared think about, and he was beginning to enjoy it.

"Andi," he called, "it's beautiful up here.

Andi climbed more slowly now, no longer fearful of hospital rules. This seemed like an adventure. Finally, she was on the roof with him. How could a place that looked so lovely at the top be so dreary and gloomy inside, she wondered. "It feels different up here," she said out loud, "like we were running away from Germany or something and escaped to freedom."

"Yeah," he agreed.

"Joe...did you mean what you said about my being beautiful, and having nothing to give me?"

"Yes, Andi."

"Why didn't you tell me I was beautiful that night?"

"I was really nervous. Just seeing you and knowing what you wanted scared me."

"You mean the perfect orgasm?"

"Yeah."

"But I was ready to give you my total self, my being, everything I had," whispered Andi, close to tears.

"Were you giving it to me or to an image of me?" he asked softly.

Andi said nothing, so Joe continued. "I just got the idea you never really saw me."

"But why?"

"Because you were looking at me as though I were so strong and special and I didn't feel anything like it."

"What did you feel?" asked Andi, with an interest she never experienced before.

"Like I really couldn't handle it. Everything was happening too fast. It was as though I was in a movie, but no one gave me the script. You assumed I knew what to say and do, but I didn't."

"Why weren't you honest then, like now?"

"Because I was too ashamed."

"So, instead you shamed me by telling me to go," said Andi quietly.

"I never thought of it that way," he admitted.

"Whether you like it or not, I don't know if I'll ever forgive you for the way you made me feel that night, but I agree that we were moving too fast."

Joe was sure that she was no longer angry with him. In fact, she was more relaxed than he ever thought she would be. So he felt comfortable saying what he thought most of his friends would probably laugh at, "Andi, I think we tried to substitute sex for feelings and that doesn't work. It took me a long time to figure this whole thing out. At first I thought I wasn't man enough and just felt ashamed. I even asked Karen out to try to forget about you. But I missed you so much, I couldn't stop thinking about you. All my running away just made me feel worse. That's what made me come here to see you and talk honestly about how I feel."

Andi stared wide eyed. She didn't know what to say. They never spoke so intimately before, but it felt good.

She looked very new and beautiful to him, and after a moment he continued, "I said I didn't think I needed forgiveness, but now I think I want it. I'm sorry I caused you so much shame."

"I can forgive you for everything except not talking to me, when I called you from the hospital," said Andi in a very even voice. "That hurt is beyond repair."

"But is it beyond our friendship?"

Andi couldn't believe her ears. Joe absolutely never talked like this before. They never had any conversation half so deep. It was as though the question formed itself and came from someone else's voice, "Are you seeing a shrink too?"

"Yes Andi, I am."

"Do you talk about us?"

"Yeah."

His admission allowed her to cross the gulf to her most extreme vulnerability, and she was finally able to ask what she knew she needed to ask from the beginning. "Should we maintain a friendship which causes us so much pain?"

"Yes, Andi, I think we should. I miss our closeness and the way we were both special for each other. It wasn't our friendship that hurt you so much as my being a coward and pushing you away."

"That's what made me want to kill myself."

"Slitting your wrists must be the loneliest feeling in the world. When I first heard about what you did, I was mad at you for wanting to die. I didn't want to think about it. I was afraid to."

"I guess that's another reason why you didn't want to talk to me when I called from the hospital."

"That's also why I forced myself to go to parties, but they only made me feel worse. Seeing the other kids always reminded me that you weren't there. And when they played our favorite songs, I couldn't stand it."

Andi was silent, but tears streamed down her cheeks. For the first time, they shared the emptiness that they could never voice. She remembered her early days in the hospital, when she kept repeating the words to their favorite songs. "Those songs helped me when I first arrived here," she finally said. "They reminded me of you."

"It's not easy to be honest Andi, but I think this is a start. I'm really glad I came."

217

Andi was about to agree with him when she spotted a group moving toward them. "My parents are here," she gasped.

"Don't panic," said Joe, quietly assessing the situation. "I'll handle it." But how, he wondered, as Mrs. Levy approached.

CHAPTER 36

The office was the usual mess. Routine was an ideal that was never achieved. Instead, chaos was the rule and Bliss immersed herself in it. But she was as shaken in the past few days as she was during her divorce. The uncertainty now was even greater. Why did I trust him, she chastised herself. Nothing in my personal life ever works. Personal life; that's a joke.

Well, if you're so upset then call him, she told herself.

Absolutely not. I knew this would happen.

Then shut up and do your work, she screamed at herself and tried to concentrate on the portfolio in front of her.

"Bliss, you're needed in the conference room," called Allison, her secretary.

"Thanks," she said, grateful for the interruption.

"Pick up line two," chimed the secretary's voice once again.

"Bliss...," came a tentative voice over the phone.

"Marty..." she honestly didn't know how to respond to him after three weeks of not hearing from him.

From outside the door, Allison called again, "Bliss, they're waiting for you."

"I can't talk, Marty. I have a conference."

"Let's meet at the duck pond near your office."

"Has anything changed?"

"As far as my marital status?"

"Yes."

"Not exactly."

"Then why bother?"

As soon as the words were out of her mouth, she knew she would give in. She always did.

"I really need to talk to you."

"Has your phone been disconnected for three weeks?"

"No, but it's been rough. Anne knows about us."

"And you promised to be a good boy," she said and hated herself.

From outside the door, Allison was insistent, "Bliss, they're buzzing for you."

"Look, I really have to go."

"Please, let's meet for lunch at the pond."

"O.K.," she finally said, just as she knew she would. The victim's role is hard to break, she told herself with disgust, and headed for the conference room.

The familiar faces and chatter calmed her. She put her outer self on automatic and brooded about Marty. So his wife finally knows, she thought. I wonder how that happened. I'm sure he never told her himself. Strange that he said his relationship with her hasn't changed. I guess they agreed to patch things up. So why the hell is he calling me, she practically screamed into the meeting.

"Because he can't stand the uncertainty any more than you can," came a voice seated directly across from her. "Our clients expect us to decrease their anxiety, not to heighten it," continued the woman. "Don't you agree, Bliss?"

"Obviously," answered Bliss, and hoped she sounded credible. How did she get into my thoughts like that, Bliss wondered. But she's right. Endings are just as important as beginnings. The final words are still unsaid and Marty needs to say them. Who knows, she almost laughed ironically, the final blows may be just as exciting as the first kiss.

"But who needs the aggravation," intoned a disgruntled voice next to her.

"Aggravation?" asked Bliss in amazement.

"Yeah, that Harbinger account is a real bitch."

"True, true," Bliss answered in her automatic voice. This is uncanny, she thought. Why are my feelings constantly bouncing back at me?

*   *   *   *

Bliss approached the park slowly. She spotted Marty almost immediately. He was already seated on a bench eating a hot dog. Just the sight of him upset her, and she knew it would be an ugly scene. Every instinct told her to leave, but she continued forward.

"I'm sorry. I should have called earlier," he offered immediately. But she had no interest in pleasantries.

"Why did you come back the night I kicked you out? It hurt like hell to tell you to leave. I wanted to chase after you, follow you down the stairs and drag you back into my apartment. But I didn't. It took all my strength to allow our relationship to end...and then you were back. Back to take whatever I had left to give. And like a fool, I gave it to you. And now like an even bigger..."

Just then his beeper went off. "I'm sorry. I have to take the call," he said weakly.

How she hated that thing. Her words froze in her mouth and her vision blurred. Yet even through her tears, she glimpsed his relief as he dialed his cell phone.

She walked to the edge of the pond and crumbled part of her sandwich to feed the ducks. They ate her bread, but it offered no comfort. She hated herself for even waiting.

"I have to leave," he finally mumbled joining her near the pond. There's an emergency at the hospital."

"Oh really," she answered with barely composed sarcasm.

"Yeah, a sixteen year old is missing."

"How convenient."

Marty recalled how the beeper once startled them from sleep as they lay on the kitchen floor in the twilight of her apartment.

"Why are you staring into space?" she demanded.

"I was remembering."

"Marty, all I've been doing for three weeks is remembering."

"Bliss, I'm sorry. But I do have this emergency. This isn't working out the way I envisioned it."

"How was that, Marty? A gallant farewell speech without the interruption of your beeper or my emotions?"

He stared at her in amazement. He really hadn't intended to say goodbye.

His silence was an insult to her, as she ripped his beeper from his belt. "There was always something between us and it was never really your wife," she screamed, jamming the beeper in his face. "As a matter of fact, your wife never interrupted us, did she? You never once thought about your wife and said you had to leave. The only thing that ever made you leave was this damned beeper." With that, she threw the beeper to the ground and began stomping it into the earth.

"Bliss, the beeper represents people who need me," said Marty through clenched teeth.

"Oh, like you really care about people. You're nothing but a joke. I can't believe you put people in touch with their feelings when you have none of your own." She paused for a moment to catch her breath, but he didn't deny her accusation.

"Why did I ever think you loved me?" she continued shrilly," and that was the last thing he heard. He tuned her out so that he could concentrate better. It was like a silent movie. Her lips were moving and her face was enraged, but he heard nothing.

She's right, he finally admitted to himself, it's over. Calling her was a mistake. I made promises we both knew I couldn't keep, but she believed them. The only remnant of her feelings is bitterness.

Bliss was furious at what appeared to be his inattention and continued her attack. "You don't even care about what I have to say. You care more about the life of this beeper than you do about mine. Your cruelty is limitless. Right now there is no one on earth I hate more than you."

A duck pecked at her foot, looking for crumbs, and Bliss paused in her tirade. She glanced from the white feathers of the duck to the tranquil water of the pond, and saw her anguish reflected in it. No, she spoke to her image, this must stop. I will not be a victim. I will not let him hurt me anymore. This thought gave her enough composure to continue.

"Your wife knows, so you dump me. How classic. And I'm supposed to accept it all, nice and sweet and ladylike."

"Bliss, I'm sorry I've caused you so much..."

"Fuck that shit," she interrupted. "You obviously don't care about me. Right now you're probably wondering if this worthless piece of metal can be salvaged," she grimaced, swooping his beeper up from the ground and holding it aloft. "Guess what? I'm going to answer that question for you immediately."

And without another word, Bliss unceremoniously flung the hated object into the water. The act assuaged her pride, and she summoned enough presence of mind to turn from him and walk away. Marty watched her leave, wondering if he would ever see her again, and then he headed for the hospital.

CHAPTER 37

Zemmel was prepared for an emergency, but the turmoil he encountered on the fourth floor was almost apocalyptic. It seemed there was little difference between patients, orderlies, nurses and doctors. How will I sort through this chaos, he questioned himself, and noted that the ward reminded him of his scene with Bliss.

Within moments, however, the situation was somewhat clarified for him by Sherrine MacIntyre. Andi Levy was on the roof, but she wasn't suicidal. Rather, she was with her boyfriend, Joe. They apparently needed the space and they took it. This was all accomplished with the help of Tina Major who, along with Andi, managed to usurp the entire authority of the fourth floor. Walking next to Zemmel, Sherrine was in tears, "I didn't think they'd be back from the hike so soon, so I was ten minutes late getting back to my post."

Zemmel paid little attention to her tears. "This is constantly happening with Andi Levy," he complained. No matter how I structure her therapy, she always manages to do exactly as she pleases." Privately he wondered if some of the blame was his. Perhaps I should have arranged a meeting between Andi and Joe in a controlled setting, he admonished himself.

"Her parents are up there with them," Sherrine continued when he paused.

"I suppose you could certainly define this as a mental health crisis," he remarked. "By the way, why aren't you with them?"

"I was, but I came down to let you know what was going on. Although the situation's bizarre, it appears stable. I made a judgment call that it was safe to leave.

"Oh," answered Marty wryly.

"There they are," said Sherrine, as she and Zemmel stepped onto the hospital rooftop.

The complete quiet of the roof struck Zemmel immediately. There was Andi with a young man, whom he surmised was Joe. Next to them were Sarah and Ed. All were seated cross legged in a corner area that overlooked the park next door. When he saw the park, Zemmel was reminded of Bliss once again.

"They seem calmer than anyone downstairs," Zemmel commented to Sherrine, "but that can change easily. As a matter of fact, a mood swing could occur momentarily. We are dealing with several volatile personalities here. Right now let's work to diffuse the situation as quickly as possible. But don't overreact. Remember, hysteria on our part could lead to a tragedy up here."

Andi was the first to spot Zemmel, and was immediately hit with mixed emotions. First there was warmth, and then there was fear. She was very happy, and she wanted to share her happiness with her doctor. Andi saw him as the one who helped her to live till this moment; the one who encouraged her when she wished she were dead. Most importantly, he was the one who was helping her to grow up.

So when she saw him, she wanted to dash over to him, throw her arms around his neck and scream, 'This is Joe. Isn't he terrific?' She really wanted his approval. She really wanted him to say everything was fine. But at the same time, she believed he would not approve. In fact this was the opposite of all his rules; the same rules that had helped her to start living again. So she remained in limbo and waited to see what would happen.

Zemmel decided to relax the situation with some humor. "We're a little close to the edge," he chuckled. "Hi, Ed and Sarah," he nodded to the Levys, and then extended his hand to Joe. "I'm Dr. Zemmel. You must be Joe. I've certainly heard a lot about you."

"I hope you're not angry with me, Dr. Zemmel," said Andi softly, "but you did tell me to think for myself."

"True," said Zemmel with a certain amount of irony in his voice.

"I've been doing it all afternoon and it feels terrific."

Zemmel was sure her attitude was truly positive, but he was still concerned with a mood swing because Andi's emotions were so intense. He signaled to Sherrine to start shepherding them in the direction of the door as the conversation progressed.

"It's our fault they came up here, Dr. Zemmel," offered Sarah. "Andi was trying to avoid her father and me."

"That's right," giggled Andi. "I thought my Mom would have a nervous breakdown if she found Joe here. Then you'd have both of us in the hospital."

"That would really be a loony bin," commented Joe.

The Levys both turned and stared at him.

Oh no, gulped Sherrine to herself, here comes the crisis.

"What are you staring at Ma? He's right," remarked Andi.

"Andi, are you purposely trying to hurt me?" asked Sarah, who by now was no longer following Sherrine to the door.

"Sarah," intervened Ed, for which Zemmel was grateful, "we've covered this ground before. Let's get downstairs."

"Wait Dad," said Andi, "I want Mom to know that I'm not trying to hurt her. Neither was Joe. We were just being honest. This family's been pretty crazy lately and we might as well face it. I hate it when the two of you try to pretend."

"Andi," coached Zemmel, "Remember your balance." Then he turned to Ed and Sarah. "This is rather impromptu, of course, but Andi's saying something pretty important about honesty."

"I'm calm now," said Andi, taking a breath, "let me try again. Mom and Dad, I know we were fighting a lot, and then I went completely off the wall and landed in the hospital. I know the two of you felt really awful and embarrassed about that and wished the whole thing never happened. But I don't. I'm getting to know myself in here. For the first time I'm starting to feel grown up, and that's very exciting for me."

For a moment everyone simply stared. And then Sarah went over to her daughter and hugged her. "I know you're growing up dear, but you're not the only one. We all are. It's just that you've had the courage to take the first step. I don't know why I got so upset when Joe made a joke about me. I guess this place would go bananas with both of us in here."

And then they were all hugging and walking toward the stairs. Sherrine couldn't believe her good fortune. It was starting to look pretty hairy for awhile, but she really admired the way Dr. Zemmel handled things.

Zemmel caught her look of admiration and experienced a pang of remorse. I'm a hero with clay feet, he thought. He remained on the roof and watched the group begin to go down the stairs. He heard Andi's laughter and remembered Bliss. Then he thought of Anne, and realized that it was almost as dangerous for him to be on the roof as it was for Andi and her family. He started to walk towards the stairs, keeping a safe distance between himself and the Levys. He'd had enough pressure for one day.

Zemmel was almost at his floor, when he stopped abruptly. There were Andi and Joe directly below him in the shadows. How the heck does she constantly manage to do whatever she pleases, he wondered. Where's Sherrine now? But at the same time he knew that Andi's strange meandering was her own route back to health, and that all the answers were not in psychiatric journals or little bottles of pills. From the beginning, Andi had a real sense of what she needed. She knew I respected that, he thought, which helped her to have a positive feeling about therapy.

Zemmel was unsure of his next move. Should he play doctor, give them a lecture and shoo them inside? Or, should he break his own rules and let them have a few moments? I really don't have a choice, he admitted and thought of Bliss and Anne once more. Why is my life narrowing down to such a tight space?

"I meant what I said on the roof, Joe," wafted Andi's voice from the stairs. "I'm starting to know myself inside and it's giving me a freedom I never knew before—the ability to think for myself. But it's not only about thinking. It's also about being friends. I'm really glad you came. It was the best talk we ever had."

"Andi, coming here was the scariest day of my life. I was scared of you, scared of getting caught in this place and scared of your doctor. And on top of all that, your parents showed up. But it was great. We kind of burst into another dimension; maybe it's friendship. Whatever it is, I like it."

"I think real friendship is another reality," said Andi, "and today we touched it."

His arm went around her and they kissed.

Zemmel coughed.

The three were caught in a moment in time where any word or action would be inappropriate. There were no excuses for any of them. None of them should be there, yet there they stood. Both Zemmel and Joe looked at Andi for direction. She was their nexus, their point of connection. Somehow, she must know what to do, and she did.

She laughed! And when she did, she proved one of Sam Haddad's theories. Laughter makes life better.

* * * *

Later that evening, Zemmel sat on the window sill of his office and looked out at the stars. He thought about how much progress Andi had made. He thought about Joe and the risks he had taken to see Andi. And then he thought about Ed and Sarah, and knew that their greatest strength was their ability to love each other and their daughter. He knew she would soon be home.

Finally, his thoughts turned to his own home and Anne's latest angry words rang in his ears, 'You took my love for granted.' He never answered her because he was afraid to admit he felt strongly disconnected from loving her. How do I describe this tight space to her, he asked himself. How do I tell her the marriage is suffocating—not because she's demanding, but because there's no passion.

'How could you betray me?' she demanded in his memory. Easily, he had wanted to shout and cry at the same time. Oh G-d Anne, that was the hardest realization of all—to see just how easy it was to betray you. But he knew that this brand of honesty was really cruelty, so again he said nothing. Instead, he did what he was becoming famous for—he walked away from her—the same way he walked away from Bliss.

He gazed out at the stars once more and thought about the world of endless possibilities. Desire for Bliss gripped him. The stars he saw were now the ones from Coney Island. He recalled the wildness of that night and how he ultimately ran away. Bliss was right, he thought. It wasn't because of Anne; not even after she found out. It was the frenzy of Bliss—the emotional overload.

I'm used to exploring feelings in a test tube, he reasoned with himself; not living them out in the open. The day after Coney Island was a disaster. It freaked me.

You lost your balance, mocked the stars, and you encouraged Bliss to interpret that as rejection.

Enough, decided Marty and pulled down the window shade. But his imagination was still on fire. He envisioned Joe kissing Andi on the stairs and knew himself to be a coward. They struggled hard for that kiss, he acknowledged, and left the office abruptly.

CHAPTER 38

Buzz...Buzz...Buzz...

Bliss was awakened from her daydream. Am I imagining the sound, she questioned herself. No, there it is again. She really didn't want to get up even though she had been in bed all day. She didn't even go to work. But she pushed herself to answer the door.

"Who is it?" she breathed into the box.

"It's Shira Katz."

"Shira who?"

"I'm sorry. I'm Chaim Katz's sister from the Mitzvah Campaign at the Yeshiva," said the young woman who was wearing a long denim skirt, long sleeved blouse and sneakers with knee socks.

"Oh right," said Bliss and remembered when the Hasidic students first came to her door. Marty was there. It was a painful thought.

Shira waited for Bliss to say something more, but there was only silence. So she tried again, "You ordered a box of Shabbas candles. Chaim asked me to bring it to you."

Bliss still said nothing, so Shira continued.

"Are you too busy?" she asked.

"No, just down," Bliss finally answered.

"Perhaps these candles will help," offered Shira, who Bliss now gauged as being about fifteen years old. "May I come up?"

"I guess so," Bliss answered, hesitantly. "How much are they?"

Shira ignored the question. Once upstairs, she simply handed Bliss a plain white and blue box with the words SHABBAT CANDLES marked on it. "Lighting candles brings harmony to the home," she said.

"It's only my son and myself," answered Bliss. "I'm divorced."

"It's not the size of the family that matters," continued Shira. "It's the spirit of Shabbas. Since this is Friday, why not light them tonight?"

Bliss opened the lid and peeked inside. There were 72 white candles in orderly rows staring at her. They didn't look very exciting, but she sensed an immediate feeling of security and liked it.

"My mother lit Shabbas candles," she confided in Shira. "But I never did. What about the prayer? I don't remember it."

"It's on the box," Shira answered gently. "But maybe you would like to order a siddur, I mean a prayer book, for something more permanent. My school sells everything."

"I used to pray every day and I hated it. Believe it or not, I went to Yeshiva."

"My teacher says people change," Shira said quietly.

"Tell me about it," Bliss muttered to herself and thought of Marty. "But I will admit that the literature your brother left me is kind of interesting," Bliss continued. "And your teacher's right. I have changed. Actually, I have some questions. Would you like to sit down?"

Shira sat on the edge of a kitchen chair, and pushed away some of the clutter on the table. "What are your questions?" she asked.

"Explain the line `Deep calls to deep,' in this pamphlet."

"That's a line from the psalms. Just last night my teacher spoke of it."

"What does it mean?" Bliss asked impatiently.

"It has to do with suffering," Shira answered slowly.

That certainly fits, Bliss thought. Out loud, she asked, "Suffering connected to what?"

"Connected to our exile, the time before the redemption."

"It sounds bleak. You're making me even more depressed than I was before. Even the sun disappeared." They both turned to the window and gazed at the almost unnatural gloom.

"There's both joy and sorrow in Jewish history," said Shira evenly. "I'm sorry if I made you sad. Maybe these will cheer you up." And swiftly, she reached into her book bag like a peddler from Europe, and pulled out a package of multicolored candles, which she opened and displayed on the kitchen table.

Bliss caught her breath. The yellows, oranges, pinks, and reds picked up the ray of sunlight that had just arrived from behind a cloud. It created an image of actual fire in front of her. "I forgot," she exclaimed with an actual lilt in her voice, "It's almost Chanukah."

"Next month," offered Shira. "Would you like some?"

"My son will kill me if I don't," she laughed.

"I'll take that as a yes," said Shira and prepared to write the order. There was a noise at the door. "What's that?" asked Shira.

"My son. He has his own key."

"Hi Mom," said Adam automatically. Then he spotted Shira and burst out laughing. "You again," the two young people said at once.

Bliss looked at her son and was glad he was laughing. She knew that he was disturbed by her unhappiness. Then she wondered how they knew each other, and realized that she didn't know who all of Adam's friends were, especially his girl friends.

"Would you two like to go into the living room and talk?" she asked.

"I have to go," said Shira blushing.

"Ma," said Adam feeling embarrassed, "Shira's very religious."

"I'm sorry, Shira," said Bliss with genuine regret, "I didn't mean to offend you."

"That's O.K. But I've got to be going. I have to help my mother get ready for Shabbas."

"Mm, when's candle lighting?" asked Bliss almost cheerfully.

"Five forty-four this evening," answered Shira.

Just then, Adam noticed the array of tiny colored candles on the kitchen table. "Wow Ma, Shira really got to you."

"Let's say she came at just the right time," said Bliss with a half smile.

Adam saw it and was grateful. He knew his Mom wasn't too happy these last few days. But all he said was, "Chanukah candles—this house is finally starting to feel like a home again."

"That's what it's all about," laughed Shira.

Shira's warmth was contagious and Bliss felt a little stronger. Although she was still unhappy, she was less overwhelmed. She looked at the simple white Shabbat candles and realized they gave her hope. It's about faith, she thought to herself.

When Shira left, Bliss turned to her son, "I know you usually like to go out on Friday night, but let's eat together tonight."

"Sure Ma," he answered. "Sounds like the old Shabbat meal they always talk about at Hebrew School."

"How do you know Shira?" asked Bliss.

"Through her brother Chaim. He's an aid with me at the Hebrew School. Sometimes Shira helps out too. By the way, what's for dinner?"

"Manicotti...Do you like her?"

"Yeah, but we come from two different worlds. Ma don't bug me. What are we having besides manicotti?"

"How about tossed salad and garlic bread?"

"This doesn't sound like the Shabbat meal Hebrew School teachers talk about," he quipped, "but it's O.K." Then he took a gulp and said, "You seem happier."

"I guess I've been poor company," she said quietly.

"Mm."

"I didn't even go to work today."

"I noticed you were still in bed when I left for school. What's going on Ma?"

"You know that guy I've been seeing?"

"Marty?"

"Yeah...it's over."

233

"I didn't like him anyway."

"You're sweet Honey, but I made a real fool of myself."

"Ma, I don't want to hurt your feelings, but I really don't want to hear the gory details. Why don't you call your friend, Carrie, or a shrink or something?"

"Call a shrink," Bliss laughed ruefully to herself. "That's a good one."

"What are you muttering about?"

"Nothing. Go do what you have to do."

"O.K. Since we're having a special meal, make dessert. And Ma, I love you."

"Thanks Adam. I needed that. I love you too," she said and gave him a kiss. "Now get out of here before I get too mushy."

Bliss filled a large pot with water and put it on the stove to boil. Then she turned to take vegetables from the refrigerator to make a salad. But she opened the refrigerator door, and closed it immediately. Salad reminded her of Marty and the dinners she prepared for him. She wanted to go into her room and throw herself on the bed.

"Ma, make brownies," came Adam's voice.

"O.K.," she answered softly and forced herself to begin making the salad. Think of Adam, she told herself. It's been rough for him. He's looking forward to a good supper and a mother who's not a zombie. As she chopped the carrots, Bliss remembered Shabbas as a child and how boring it was. She couldn't wait for it to be over. I must have changed, she thought, glancing at the box of Shabbat candles, because now I can hardly wait for it to start.

Funny how Adam referred to a Shabbat meal so whimsically, Bliss continued her reverie. We had them every week and the routine was stifling. Always the same meal. I vowed to be different and now my son yearns for it all, she acknowledged ironically. He'd probably give anything for chicken soup, she thought, and almost wished she could make some. Then cook up some split pea soup, she told herself. Adam really likes it.

So did Marty, she recalled. But the thought of Marty did not make her feel like disintegrating quite so much this time. Forget what Marty liked, she advised herself. <u>You</u> like split pea soup. Focus on that. It's true, she thought, sorting through the peas. I like cooking it and eating it. Just then a curious thought struck her.

"Guess what!" she called to Adam. "I never ordered Shabbas candles or anything else from those kids. I wonder why Shira came."

"That's what's great about Chaim and Shira," Adam called back, "They're always at the right place at the right time. They have some weird sounding Jewish word for it. It means divine providence."

"Very interesting," commented Bliss and threw the peas into boiling water. "Kind of makes you feel like maybe there's a reason for all the aggravation. It was perfect timing the way she showed up."

"If you say so," agreed Adam. "I gotta go now. Remember, bake brownies...and don't burn the garlic bread."

"O.K., O.K., but be back for candle lighting time. It's important to me."

Bliss heard the door slam after her son and some of the empty feelings returned. But she felt better than earlier in the day. I can cope, she told herself, and began stuffing the manicotti shells with a ricotta mixture.

"What's that smoke?" she screeched, and realized it was the garlic bread. Why do I always let it burn, she admonished herself and felt like tears. Stop it, she commanded herself. You can handle it.

Bliss finally got the manicotti in the oven and remembered the candles. Well, she thought, if I'm lighting candles and having a Shabbat meal, I want to make it beautiful. The first thing I need are candlesticks.

There must be a pair somewhere around here. Mom always made sure I had them. Bliss looked under a pile of junk in a back closet but found nothing. What about on top, she wondered. There were no candlesticks, but there was a hand stitched tablecloth that she immediately knew would be perfect for the dining room table.

You're eating in the dining room, asked a voice in her head.

Yes, she answered with more confidence than she experienced in awhile. I'm making a special Shabbat meal for Adam and myself.

She spread the faded but aristocratic looking tablecloth on the dining room table, and was suddenly sure she knew where the candlesticks were—the cupboard under the sink.

Sure enough, there they were. Hmm, Bliss thought, they look like artifacts from a Peruvian find. The silver was all tarnished and mottled. They sure are old and ugly looking, she thought, but I like that. I don't feel very shiny, bright and new either. Actually, their age gave Bliss a feeling of continuity. Like maybe there was a reason and a place for everything—even the painfully ugly aspects of life.

Stop being so morbid, admonished the voice in her head. All you need to do is polish the candlesticks and they'll look terrific. Bliss found the silver polish and a rag. She remembered the way her father always stood behind her mother when her mother lit the candles. Bliss never paid much attention. It was all part of the scenery of the rather meaningless part of her childhood. I never thought my mother had much, she thought with some bitterness, but I have even less. Again she came close to tears.

Stop that, isn't it almost time to light the candles, came the voice, that Bliss finally recognized as her mother's.

Mm hum, Bliss almost answered, and put the finishing touches on her silver polishing. Then she straightened the tablecloth and set the candlesticks on it. Hurriedly, she found matches and inserted the candles into the little holders. She paused to admire her work, when her mother's voice asked, where's Adam?

Oh no, Bliss thought, where is he? I told him to be home. Just then, the lock clicked. "Adam, you made it. Come in," she called and struck the match.

"Take it easy. You don't have to yell," Adam complained, walking into the house, but he paused when he saw Bliss, who was already lighting the second Shabbat candle. Then without looking at the box for help, she recited the ancient *bracha* from childhood memory.

"Shabbat Shalom," she said, turning to her son with a smile.

"Shabbat Shalom," Adam grinned back, "where's the food?"

"Adam, do you ever think about poetry?" asked Bliss as she served the soup.

"Not usually," answered her son after he picked up a slice of garlic bread, and began scraping off some of the burnt part.

"I don't mean in a poem. I mean in life. Sometimes you try to reach for something beautiful—that's what I mean by poetry."

"I know," Adam brightened with comprehension. "Like when you lit the candles. It was very quiet and you looked peaceful. It reminded me of a painting. Is that what you mean by poetry?"

Bliss stared at Adam. He was amazingly intuitive. Why hadn't they talked in such a long time?

"Wake up, Ma, the phone's ringing," shrieked Adam, unable to comprehend why his mother didn't move to pick up the receiver at her elbow.

"We're not answering," Bliss informed him with resolve, "it's Shabbat."

CHAPTER 39

Marty lay sprawled on a recliner in his den. The T.V. was on, but he wasn't watching. Instead, his eyes wandered to the fish tank on the opposite side of the room. These were the only living creatures to share his privacy. Anne hated the dingy quality of the smoky walls and never entered the room. Marty enjoyed the assurance of her absence.

There were five fish in the ten gallon fish tank. He looked very hard at the fish, and saw them as prisoners caught in a world of glass that limited their movement to a desperately small few cubits. What are their choices, he asked himself, and wondered about his own.

Still looking at the fish, he reached for the phone at his elbow and dialed. He heard the ringing, but could not accept that there was no answer. She's got to be there, he told himself. Where the hell would she be? Answer you bitch, he muttered into the line. I've got to talk to you. This isn't fair. Why can't you ever listen?

"Dad, get off the phone," Allen burst into the room, carrying a bottle of pills. "Mom's out cold. It looks like she took these and there's an empty bottle of scotch by her bed. We've got to call an ambulance."

Marty stared dumbfounded at the vial of Prozac that Allen thrust at him. He always prescribed it for Anne when she complained about feeling depressed, but he knew he should have kept closer track of her after she found out about Bliss. He wanted to rush to her, to beg forgiveness, to make everything fine—but his feet wouldn't move. They were immobile, while he concentrated on his son's voice, as he spoke to intake at the Emergency Room.

"Anne Zemmel...52...she took pills...Prozac, and apparently she was drinking at the same time. She's completely unconscious...Dad, how many do you think she took tonight?...Dad, answer me!"

"Uh, I'm not sure."

"We're not sure," said Allen with bitter irony. "My father's a doctor. He prescribed them himself. The address is 38 Old Notch Hills Road in Short Hills...I can't speak about anything right now. I don't live here anymore. I was only stopping by to see my Mom...You're asking me questions I can't answer. I knew she was really down, but I don't know the details. You really need to talk to my father...Dad...Dad..."

Without looking up, Allen instinctively knew his father was gone. "Look, how soon will they be here?...Thank you. I'm sorry, but I can't talk," he hurriedly spoke into the phone and hung up. "Dad, you bastard, where the hell are you?" he muttered through clenched teeth and ran to sit beside his mother.

Anne stirred slightly at his presence. "Hang on Ma," he whispered to her, "I'm right here with you. Soon the ambulance will be here." Then he stroked her hand and was silent.

Their repose was shattered by sirens and flashing lights. Anne was quickly placed on a stretcher. "Will you ride in the ambulance or follow?" asked a concerned voice.

"I'll follow," answered Allen, his face wet.

Allen watched the medics put his mother in the ambulance and then turned to lock the door. He was startled by Marty approaching the front steps.

"Where were you?" he asked his father, with barely controlled anger.

"In my car. I couldn't take it in there."

"What about her? Don't you think she needed you?"

"I'm not sure she wanted to see me."

"You really have an answer for everything," spat Allen contemptuously. "How could you give her a refillable prescription in her state of mind. That was like handing her a shotgun."

"Allen, let's not do this."

"Dad, I'm looking for answers, not shrink talk."

"I think you already know the answer," said Marty. "I'm guilty."

"How can you be so cool even now," asked Allen, enraged. "Yes, I know the answer. I've known it for almost as long as she has. But I thought you might have some decency in you. Something to give her now."

"I wish I did, Allen, but betrayal is not easily undone."

"G-d, you say it so coldly, so remorselessly. Are you human? Are you actually my father? You lousy hypocrite!"

Marty turned away from Allen's glare. He reached for words to make it better; words he didn't have. And then his son was gone.

Allen's car roared away and Marty stood in its wake. He watched the trail of exhaust as the car disappeared from view, and continued reverberating from the anger and bitterness that permeated his relationship with his son. The hateful conversation they just had was not foreign to them, but it was even more painful tonight. Anne was the strength that connected them no matter how alienated they became from each other. And now even that channel was collapsed.

Allen wants answers, thought Marty ruefully, and he probably deserves them. But I don't deal in answers. I seek to follow patterns and then to understand them. He would call that cold and unfeeling. Take it as a rejection of himself. The same way Anne did. The way Bliss did.

Marty knew himself to be totally alone at that moment. Not so much because his wife was on her way to the hospital, his son had just denounced him and his lover refused to answer her phone, but because he could not convey feeling to any one of them. He stood outside of them and outside of himself.

And yet he admitted the aloneness was appealing. He needed the detachment to trace the pattern, to hold it close and to examine it. I'm filling my space with no one but me, he thought, and began to meditate.

He visualized his separateness from others; his alienation. A great sadness overtook him, but from within that sadness his concentration grew strong. This time, when he focused on his severed ties, he was able to perceive Anne's humiliation. And from the depth of her humiliation, he recognized an image.

With the ambulance siren still ringing in his ears, he pictured Anne sitting alone in their outdoor Jacuzzi with a glass in her hand. It was the omnipresent drink that captured his attention. The drink I chose to ignore, he accused himself. She was crying for help and all I did was write more prescriptions.

He easily spied into the underpinnings of Anne's unhappiness and the pieces of her mosaic began to make sense. She's been crying out to me for years...It started with Allen. No, he paused with nearly unbearable insight, this goes beyond Allen. And I ignored her.

The honesty of his last thought was a powerful catalyst to Marty's concentration. Shock waves went through his nervous system and he entered not only Anne's consciousness, but his own.

I never believed any knowledge would come through her, he realized in a trance. I always thought Bliss would lead me to this. She was much more outspoken about the truth. But there was no time for speculation. Marty visualized the last stone falling neatly into place, and saw with unerring clarity exactly what a shit he actually was.

CHAPTER 40

By Sunday morning, Marty was stale and unkempt. His skin was sallow and his beard was stubble because he'd forgotten to shave. He left the house with no clear idea about where to go. It was only when he got behind the steering wheel that he thought of the gym. He focused on the punching bag as he headed in the direction of Jersey City. All he wanted to do was batter the bag and smash his present reality out of existence.

In the parking lot, he took his extra gym bag out of the trunk and headed for the lockers with a vengeance. First I'll do a series of situps and pushups, he decided. Then I'll run around the track. I need to get the knots out.

Marty ran till he was exhausted and even jumped some rope before he went over to the punching bag. He was so immersed in himself that he didn't notice the man alongside him until a rapid cadence of punches caught his ear. This guy's reaction time is great, Marty thought and began to introduce himself.

"Hi, I'm Marty Zemmel."

The man paused and turned around, "I'm Baruch Yehudi," he answered, and gave Marty a warm handshake.

Only then did Marty notice the yarmulke that covered most of the man's head. Baruch responded to Marty's open stare cheerfully. "I'm the new director of the Jewish Chabbad House down the street. We run an alcohol and drug treatment program for the neighborhood."

Marty immediately wondered at the connection between this and Anne, but only asked, "Is it for Jews and non-Jews?"

"Certainly," answered Baruch.

The two men said nothing else and continued punching the bags in front of them.

"What's your line?" Baruch finally asked.

"I'm a shrink," said Marty as simply as possible. He really didn't want to be plagued by questions about Freud, Jung or crackpot theories, but he wasn't prepared for Baruch's silence.

"Is that a problem for you?" Marty finally asked.

"No, I'm just amazed to find another shrink in a place like this," Baruch answered quietly. "Wanna spar?"

"Sure," answered Marty, infused by an electrical charge, as they walked towards the ring.

"Strange coincidences," remarked Baruch as they stepped through the ropes and into the ring.

The two men sparred lightly, each interested in knowing more about the other.

"More than you think," said Marty, deciding to be candid. "You work with substance abusers, and on Friday night my wife O.D.'d on a prescription drug I provided for her. She was also drinking."

That explains his anxiety, thought Baruch, dodging Marty's right hook. "Would you like to come to our house and talk?" he asked, throwing a punch that caught Marty on the chin.

Marty knew that even a week ago he would have refused such an invitation, but now there was nowhere else to go. "O.K.", he answered, and this time his right hook landed on target.

* * * *

Marty and Baruch were seated in the large, old fashioned kitchen of the Chabad House. A wood-burning fireplace stood in a corner of the room. Across from it were a double sink and a huge greasy stove. Built into an adjacent wall were cupboards with the words, "Meat" and "Dairy" neatly written in black magic marker.

"Would you like some coffee," asked Baruch, seated across from Marty at a kitchen table covered by an old oil cloth.

Marty was reminded of Bliss. She always offered him coffee. And from there he free associated to Chaim Katz. There's something eerie about the way everything is connecting, he thought. But all he said was, "Thanks, that'll be fine."

"You seem preoccupied," observed Baruch.

"I am."

"About your wife?"

"Among other things."

Both men fell silent. Baruch finally realized that Marty wasn't just a frantic husband. His distress went deeper than that.

"Oddly enough," Marty continued tentatively, "I've been hounded by people like you for the past few months." The subject both intrigued and frightened him, and he stopped abruptly.

"You mean Torah outreach people?" offered Baruch.

"Mm...Up until now I've refused to involve myself with them."

"And now?"

"Now it looks like I'm in the middle of their inner sanctum," Marty laughed weakly, and pointed to the signs proclaiming meat and dairy, the double sink and the daily prayer books strewn all over the counter tops.

"Although I'm not a believer in traditional Judaism," continued Marty, "I think our encounter has a mystical quality to it. I have a strong sense that I'm supposed to be here...to talk with you."

"So talk."

"I'm at the bottom of my life," began Marty candidly. "And I feel nothing. Everyone expects reactions from me that I can't give. My wife just overdosed on pills, and all I can think about is my professional accountability because I prescribed them without monitoring her. My son branded me as a hypocrite and he's right. But again, I don't care."

"Is that all you don't care about?" asked Baruch carefully.

"There's a woman...somewhat younger than myself. She also wanted what I couldn't give."

"You mean feelings?"

"No, commitment." Marty paused and looked into Baruch's eyes which suddenly appeared to be accusing him. They're like laser beams, he thought noting his paranoia and a wanton desire to punch Baruch's face.

Instead, he pounded the table with his fist. "I was in love," he began to sob. "Does that make me a criminal? A law breaker? A breaker of your damned religious antiquated laws...Oh, pardon me," continued Marty sarcastically, "I forgot. This is a holy place."

"This is a place where people come to express very sad and unhappy feelings, just like you're doing."

"I said I had no feelings."

"I thought you said you were in love?"

Marty flushed. "Looks like you just put me in checkmate."

"Perhaps I went too far. You have my apologies."

"No, it's O.K. I need to talk. I saw myself so clearly Friday night. The whole story - my wife, my son, myself. It was so apparent, so perfect. It's driving me crazy. I have to tell someone."

"I'm listening."

"As I already mentioned, I was disconnected from feelings— estranged from everyone. But in that moment of isolation, outside in the dark, after my son helped my wife into the ambulance and I did absolutely nothing to comfort her or help her, I actually connected up to myself..."

"Go on."

"I saw myself more clearly than ever in my entire life. And do you know what I saw?" Marty was shouting by now, "I saw I was shit! Pure unadulterated shit. That's my feeling."

"It's a start...would you like a glass of water?"

"Thanks, I would...You know," Marty laughed nervously, "I feel like the shrink in the comics...nuttier than the patients."

"And just as powerless," said Baruch as he went to the sink to get Marty his water.

"So what do you prescribe?" asked Marty, taking a drink and starting to unwind.

"Torah and some crisis intervention."

"Torah," snorted Marty disparagingly. "How can Torah take away my despair?"

"It's never easy to find joy in despair. But with proper interpretation and guidance, the Torah leads people into a healthier mode and a positive lifestyle."

"Well," Marty conceded grudgingly, "I guess you would need some highly complex interpretations."

"You're quite right," agreed Baruch, "and our interpretations are not only complex, but inspired."

"Where does all this come from?" Marty laughed in spite of himself, actually charmed by Baruch's enthusiasm.

"Interpretations of Torah have been handed down through the ages, but our inspiration comes from the Rebbe."

Marty's smile died on his lips. "Are you talking about that manipulator in Crown Heights?"

"Why do you call him that?" asked Baruch with raised eyebrows.

"Because he's always busy pulling strings. If the Torah's so great, why can't people find their own joy in it. Why does he have to put his stamp of approval on everything?"

"The Torah is great but we are not. What you call a stamp of approval is what we call a blessing."

"And what gives him the right to give out all the blessings?"

"You'll have to see for yourself," said Baruch very simply.

"Are you suggesting that I go to the Rebbe?" Marty exploded. "With all your medical background, the only advice you can give me is a trip to the Rebbe?"

"Do you have any better ideas?"

Marty was silent, so Baruch continued. "Take a ride to Crown Heights. The Rebbe's giving out dollars to everyone who visits him today and the blessing's included at no extra charge. The waiting line is only about two hours."

"Are you serious? Don't you see how beat I am? All you can tell me is to stand on line?"

"That's not all I'm telling you. Of course, I'd like to continue this dialogue and offer you my expertise if you want it. But for me, a blessing from the Rebbe is part of that process."

Marty looked at Baruch's truly caring face and knew the psychiatrist meant well, but was missing the point.

"I don't want to see some dried up old guy. I want to feel young and vigorous. That's why I work out in the gym and that's why I pursued..."

"That woman."

"Mm hum."

So that's it, realized Baruch, the eternal conflict between youth and age. What else can I say to him?

They stared at each other awkwardly. The allusion to Bliss caused Marty to long for her touch once more. I've gotta get out of here, he thought. But where am I going? It's over with Bliss. I know she won't see me.

"You look kind of pale," commented Baruch. Can I get you something else?"

"No, no thanks. I just feel like I've gotta be on the move...but thanks for providing the space," Marty rose from the table and extended his hand, "I needed it."

"Please come again," said Baruch. "I've enjoyed our talk and I'd like to tell you more about the Rebbe. He sees hundreds of people a day you know."

At that moment, Marty envisioned a bearded old man giving out dollars all day. It actually seemed comical, rather than threatening. In fact, it's downright altruistic, he thought. "You win," he finally said. "Perhaps I've misjudged things. One of these days, I just might check him out."

"Don't make it one of these days. Make it today."

For the first time, Marty noticed the flaming idealism in Baruch Yehudi's eyes. That's the look I used to see in Anne, he remembered. And now there's just a vast emptiness. He thought again about where to go next and came up with zero. Maybe the Rebbe isn't such a bad idea, he decided. At least it's a destination.

"O.K. Baruch," Marty said, I'll go. I don't like your rule book, but I like your passion and sense of mysticism. And I appreciate the way you let me sit here and cry...Thanks. I'll be back."

Marty walked down the rather long and dark hallway that led to the outside. He blinked in the sunlight and walked to his car. Then he headed for Brooklyn. He knew it wasn't just for a lack of anything better to do, and it wasn't for the dollar either.

It's for the hope, thought Marty. There was an unspoken promise in Baruch's eyes. That's why I'm going.

Although Marty did not know the specific location of the Rebbe, he found him with little difficulty. His approach to Eastern Parkway was soon marked by a long line of people waiting to get into a large brownstone building. This must be it, he thought, and parked the car.

*   *   *   *

"Relax, don't push," came a voice from behind Marty, while someone else elbowed his back.

"Is it always like this?" Marty asked the black-hatted man next to him who was lurching forward.

"Today's a little worse than usual."

"How often do you come?" asked Marty.

"Maybe once a week, if I can make it."

"Get back, you're stepping on my foot," came a shout from behind.

Marty turned and saw a sea of black hats that seemed to extend for blocks. He realized that he was squeezed so tightly he couldn't leave. There was no choice but to go forward.

Inside the building the standing people grew quieter. It wasn't quite as cramped, but it was still congested. The hallways were narrow and filled to capacity with wall-to-wall people. Marty prevented a choking spasm by popping a cough drop and taking a shallow breath.

The hush intensified as the line slowly progressed toward the Rebbe. People grew more expectant with each footfall. "Think of what you want to say to him," a father whispered to his son.

Marty was now four people away from the Rebbe, a black-hatted, bearded, ninety-year-old man with piercing blue eyes, who rested his body rather heavily on a low wooden podium. All that could be heard was the slight rustle of quickly dispersed dollar bills, and the soft slur of Yiddish that went with them.

Two feet from the Rebbe stood a man who directed people toward the exit, as soon as they received their Rebbe Dollars. He was ramrod straight and reminded Marty of a drill sergeant. "Move along," he beckoned routinely.

And then it was Marty's turn to see the Rebbe. He stood before the frail wise man and stared. Before he knew what was happening, the dollar was in his hand and the Yiddish phrase was in his ear. He had no comprehension of it's meaning.

"Move along," said the drill sergeant next to the Rebbe, but Marty didn't respond.

"People are waiting," continued the voice. Still Marty didn't move. Is this all there is, he thought in a daze. There's got to be more.

The drill sergeant opened his mouth to repeat his order more sharply, but immediately closed it. The Rebbe was extending one finger of his right hand toward Marty. "Venez plus pres" he said very clearly.

It took a moment for Marty to register that the Rebbe was talking to him in French. How does he know I speak French, he wondered, as he stepped forward. And then the two men were staring at each other. The Rebbe nodded and continued in French. "Votre femme est tres malade. Prenez-lui cet argent," he said, and placed a second dollar in Marty's hand.

Questions jammed Marty's brain. He wanted to ask the Rebbe how he knew about Anne. Trembling, Marty began to formulate words, but the old bearded wise man was already looking to the next person, a new dollar poised in the air.

"Give two of your own dollars to charity," advised the drill sergeant, and guided Marty to the next room. Marty fumbled for his wallet and placed some bills into a box marked for the handicapped. "How did he know?" Marty asked the elderly man holding the metal box.

"You mean, the Rebbe?"

"Yes."

"How could he not know?" asserted the old man, "He's the Rebbe."

Marty quickly left the building. The brisk Crown Heights air hit him full in the face, but he didn't notice it. Everything looked blurry. His brain sang with the Rebbe's words: 'Your wife is very sick. Take this to her.'

In fact, Anne's dollar seemed like it was burning into Marty's skin. Maybe I should throw it away, he thought. But the Rebbe knew about Anne's sickness, Marty countered himself. He was very deliberate in the way he spoke to me. It wasn't just a lucky guess. How can I throw it away?

Marty sensed that reality as he'd always supposed it to be would never be the same. It was like blinders were being taken off and he was given new vision. But he was very uncertain about what this vision signified or how he should respond to it.

Is it really feasible for me to go and see Anne, he wondered. She's very angry with me. What if I damage her further? Marty was so lost in himself, he began to cross the street without paying attention to traffic. Cars beeped all around him.

If only this noise would disappear, wished Marty, so I could think about what's happened. He spoke to me in French, he talked about Anne's being sick. This isn't possible, yet it is. Is this what makes people turn into robots for the Rebbe? Or is there something more here that I'm missing?

Finally Marty was near his car. Standing next to it was an old woman with a kerchief on her head, begging for money. Marty gave her a few dollars. He wanted to grab her and scream, where does the Rebbe get his information? What's the secret? Does everyone know but me? But he didn't dare open his mouth because he feared what he might say or do.

Just then another pair of hands appeared. This time they belonged to a very old man in a threadbare suit holding a cigar box. "Here," said Marty, "take the five and the ten."

More hands appeared holding more charity boxes of different shapes and sizes. "Take, take," screamed Marty jamming money frantically into all the boxes until only two dollars were left. "I can't give you these," he muttered without looking at anyone in particular. "They're from the Rebbe."

"That's O.K. Mister," said a young voice, "I just saw you giving away money, so I wanted some."

"For yourself?" asked Marty, seeing the 10 year old child in front of him for the first time.

"Yeah, my Mom's laid off," the boy explained.

Marty handed him one of the bills. "You can take this, but I can't give you the other one. It's for my wife. She's in the hospital."

Marty wanted to explain more about Anne to the boy; to tell him about his years with her and the horror of those years. He wanted to talk about how they kept the horror secret; how he forbade her to mention it. But the boy was smiling and taking the money, with no comprehension of Marty's dilemma.

"Gee thanks, Mister," he said and ran off into an alleyway.

All the beggars were gone. Marty stood alone with the single bill in his hand. Take it to your wife, he heard the Rebbe's voice and felt the blue eyes piercing into him.

Marty was used to knowing what the patients sitting before him did not know. There was a power in knowledge, which he treasured immensely. That's why they see me, he always assured himself. Because I know.

Yet, for the first time in a long time, Marty was quite certain that he didn't know. In fact, the certainty of his blindness was more significant at that moment than all his previous knowledge. Maybe there's strength in not knowing, he reasoned. Because when you don't know, you exercise faith and trust beyond all prior knowledge.

By now Marty was sitting behind the wheel of his car, still unsure about where to go. He turned the key in the ignition. I'm acting on faith, he thought slowly and pressed his foot on the gas.

He leaned forward to turn on the radio and caught sight of himself in the rear view mirror. To his surprise, he looked relaxed. This is an adventure, he advised himself, and maneuvered his car into the late afternoon Crown Heights traffic.

Take the dollar to Anne; she needs you, came an insistent voice, which Marty finally realized was his own. With a new sense of humility, he understood the Rebbe's gift to him. It was courage!

Ahead of Marty a big van with the words "Mitzvah Mobile" and a picture of a huge Jewish star blared a message. To the side, beggars lined up on the corner, charity boxes extended. Several women with covered heads strolled baby carriages through the crosswalk in front of Marty, as he waited at a red light. So this is Crown Heights, he remarked to himself. I think I like it.

Marty noticed that much of his deadness was lifting. Maybe it's not too late for us to talk...really talk, he thought, and headed towards Anne.

www.ingramcontent.com/pod-product-compliance
Lightning Source LLC
Chambersburg PA
CBHW030258290526
45785CB00001B/137